TARLA DALAL'S
NEW
INDIAN
VEGETARIAN
COOKERY

TARLA DALAL'S
NEW
INDIAN VEGETARIAN COOKERY

EBURY PRESS
LONDON

Published by Ebury Press
Division of the National Magazine Company Ltd
Colquhoun House
27–37 Broadwick Street
London W1V 1FR

First Impression 1986

ISBN 085223 412 0

Editor · Maria Mosby
Editorial Assistant · Emma-Lee Gow
Designer · Ted McCausland
Photographer · Jan Baldwin
Stylists · Cathy Sinker and Tamasin Summers
Cookery · Maxine Clark

Computerset by MFK Typesetting Ltd, Hitchin, Herts.
Printed and bound in Yugoslavia by Mladinska Knjiga, Ljubljana

CONTENTS

INTRODUCTION

India, undoubtedly, has the largest population of vegetarians of any country in the world and also the widest range and number of vegetarian dishes. The types of dishes and the way in which they are prepared, however, vary significantly from region to region. Wheat breads, for example, are part of the daily meal in the North, West and East, but in the South, breads are not eaten, so rice plays a predominant role in the diet. Because of these regional variations, there is no one typical Indian vegetarian meal, although a traditional meal in most parts of the country would consist of a vegetable dish, a dal or kadhi, an accompaniment or relish, bread and/or rice. On special occasions, the meal would include savouries, sweet dishes and pullavs. In some parts of the country, buttermilk (lassi) would also be served along with the meal.

In planning a meal, the Indian cook tries to balance the dishes, by varying the colours, textures and flavours. If, for example, the vegetable is soft – like spinach – a crunchy accompaniment or relish would be served by way of contrast. If no dal is served, a mixture of pulses with sauce or a vegetable with sauce would be included. And if, as in well-to-do households, two vegetable dishes are served, one would be dry and the other accompanied by a sauce.

An important difference to Western cooking is that fresh rather than prepared ingredients are used. Canned or frozen vegetables are not a part of traditional Indian cooking, and spice powders (masalas) are always freshly ground. The eating of food is also greatly different from the West. The early Indian tradition was to serve dishes in banana leaves or in plates made of dry leaves with dry leaf cups being used for liquids. Nowadays, metal thalis (flat-bottomed plates with a shallow rim) are used together with metal katoris (straight-sided cups with no handles). Although spoons are used for liquids, raitas and sauces, knives and forks are not used, mainly because they are not suited to Indian breads. Indians eat with their hands and use them also for tearing the bread into pieces. Except in South India (where the palm is also used), only the tips of the right hand fingers are used to transfer the food to the mouth. Naturally, the hands are washed both before and after eating.

As far as kitchen equipment is concerned, only a few special utensils are used. The tawa (which is made of heavy cast iron and is similar to a griddle) is used for making chapatis, rotis and parathas. The kadai, which looks like the Chinese wok but is a little deeper, is used for frying and is also made of cast iron. A deep-fat fryer or a wok can be used instead. A mortar and pestle is used for grinding dry powders and, for making pastes, a special flat grinding stone is used together with a stone roller. In the modern kitchen, the mortar and pestle can be replaced by an electric grinder and the grinding stone by a blender. Other useful tools in the Indian kitchen include tongs for handling chapatis, parathas and other breads, and slotted spoons for removing fried food from the kadai.

In the recent past, say the last ten to twenty years, many changes have taken place. American and Italian specialities have made their appearance and fast-food chains offering hamburgers, hot dogs, pizzas (both vegetarian and non-vegetarian) have sprung up in the larger cities. The average urban housewife is anxious to learn from, and experiment with, new ideas and to simplify and shorten the preparation time of traditional Indian dishes.

In this book, I have included some traditional as well as some newer recipes to please the palates of Indians and Westerners alike. Some may find the flavours of the spices too strong or, for that matter, too mild. I am sure that you will find no problem in adjusting the quantities to suit your taste.

In conclusion, I hope and wish that this book will provide you and your family with much joy and pleasure.

REGIONAL AREAS OF INDIA

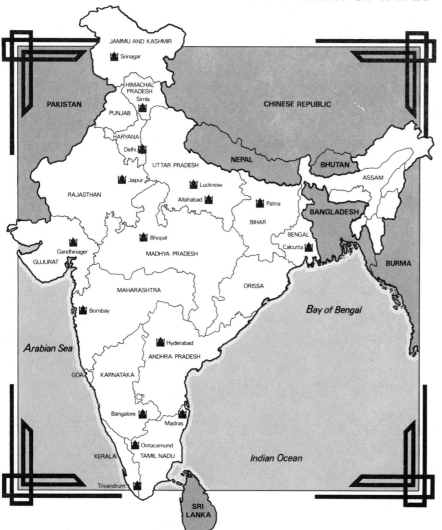

WEIGHTS AND MEASURES

Weights corresponding to 1 cup (200 ml) measure

	OZ.	G.		OZ.	G.
Almonds	5	150	Mint leaves – *fresh*	1½	40
Amchur powder	2	50	Mooli – *chopped*	4	100
Aniseed	3	75	Moong dal	6	175
Apple – *peeled and cored*	3	75	Moong sprouts	4	100
Beans, French – *chopped*	4	100	Mushrooms –		
Bean sprouts	3	75	(*canned*) *drained*	4	100
Black-eyed beans	5	150	Noodles – *fried*	2	50
Cabbage – *chopped*	3	75	Peas, green – *shelled*	4	100
grated	4	100	Peanuts	5	150
Carrots – *cubed or*			Pepper, green – *cubed*	4	100
chopped	4	100	Pistachio nuts	4	100
grated	3	75	Poppy seeds	4	100
Cashew nuts	4	100	Potatoes – *cubed*	4	100
Cauliflower florets	3	75	Potatoes – *sweet, cubed*	4	100
Chana	6	175	Rice – *cooked*	6	175
Chana dal	5	150	*raw*	6	175
Chick peas – *green*	6	175	*beaten (pohe)*	3	75
white	6	175	Salt	9	250
Chillies	1	25	Semolina	5	150
Coriander – *leaves*	1	25	Spinach – *chopped*	3	75
seeds	2	50	Spring onions – *chopped*	3	75
Creamed coconut	4	100	Sugar	5	150
Croûtons	2	50	Sweetcorn kernels	6	175
Cumin seeds	4	100	Tamarind pods	4	100
Fenugreek – *seeds*	5	150	Tomatoes – *chopped*	4	100
leaves fresh	1	25	Vegetables –		
leaves dried	1	25	*mixed, cooked*	3	75
Flour – *gram*	4	125	Yam	4	100
plain	4	125			
wholemeal	4	125			
Kidney beans, red	5	150			
Masoor dal	6	175		FL OZ.	ML.
Math sprouts	4	100	Milk – *fresh*	7	200
Milk – *dried*	3	75	Water	7	200

SOUPS

Indian cooking has a limited range of traditional soups which include the *shorbas* of the North, the *osamans* of Gujarat, the *saars* of Maharashtra and the fiery *rasams* of the South.

Recently, with the gradual spread of external influence, soups have become more popular with vegetarians and, in fact, over the last few years, packets of ready-made soups have been introduced to the Indian market.

In the cities, serving soups as light meals is becoming an increasing trend, but in the country areas of North India the tradition is to serve all dishes together in a thali or large plate, so the idea of offering soup as a separate course has not yet been adopted.

TOMATO SHORBA
Tomate che saar ◗

Serves: 4–6
Preparation time: 15 minutes
Cooking time: 15 minutes

This lovely light soup is from the region of Maharashtra.

1 kg (2¼ lb) tomatoes, roughly chopped
400 ml (⅔ pint) water
10 ml (2 tsp) gram flour (besan)
750 ml (1¼ pints) thin coconut milk, strained (page 116)
15 ml (1 tbsp) ghee (page 113) or oil
5 ml (1 level tsp) cumin seeds
3–4 curry leaves
2–3 green chillies, slit
15 ml (1 tbsp) jaggery (gur) or 10 ml (2 level tsp) sugar
salt
15 ml (1 tbsp) finely chopped fresh coriander leaves, to garnish

Put the tomatoes into a pan with the water. Bring to the boil, then simmer for 5 minutes until cooked. Purée, then strain.
   Add the gram flour to the coconut milk and mix well.
   Heat the ghee in a pan and fry the cumin seeds until they splutter. Add the curry leaves, green chillies, tomato soup, coconut milk and jaggery. Season with salt and cook for 4–5 minutes. Garnish with coriander leaves and serve hot.

PINEAPPLE RASAM
Annasi rasam ◗

Serves: 4
Preparation time: 5 minutes
Cooking time: 5 minutes

30 ml (2 level tsp) cornflour
800 ml (1⅓ pints) pineapple juice
3 black peppercorns
5 ml (1 level tsp) cumin seeds
15 ml (1 tbsp) ghee (page 113)
1 green chilli, slit
salt
15 ml (1 tbsp) finely chopped fresh coriander leaves

Stir the cornflour into the pineapple juice and set aside.
   Dry roast the peppercorns and half the cumin seeds together for a few seconds, then cool and grind to a powder.
   Melt the ghee in a frying pan and fry the remaining cumin seeds until brown. Add the pineapple juice mixture, green chilli, peppercorn powder and salt to taste, and cook for 1–2 minutes.
   Discard the chilli and pour the soup into individual serving bowls. Garnish with the coriander leaves and serve at once.

HERB SOUP
Hara shorba

An attractive green colour with a delicate flavour of mild spices, this soup is delicious served with slices of lemon.

225 g (8 oz) shelled green peas
75 g (3 oz) spinach, finely chopped
75 g (3 oz) spring onions, finely chopped
15 ml (1 tbsp) finely chopped fresh coriander leaves
6 mint leaves
1.1 litres (2 pints) water
15 ml (1 tbsp) butter
15 ml (1 level tbsp) plain flour (maida)
1 small piece nutmeg, ground
6 black peppercorns, ground
45 ml (3 tbsp) cream

Serves: 6
Preparation time: 10 minutes
Cooking time: 30 minutes

Put all the vegetables with the herbs and the water into a pan. Bring to the boil, then simmer for 10–15 minutes until the vegetables are tender. Transfer to a blender or food processor and blend to a purée.

   Melt the butter in a pan and gradually stir in the flour. Cook stirring for 30 seconds, then add the puréed vegetable mixture and the ground spices and simmer for 10 minutes.

   Beat the cream and stir into the soup to heat through or swirl into individual servings. Serve hot.

BEAN AND CHEESE SOUP
Poushtik soup

Whey is used as stock in this nourishing soup. Serve it with lemon juice.

175 g (6 oz) soft cheese (pressed paneer, page 114) and corresponding
   whey
30 ml (2 level tbsp) moong dal
175 g (6 oz) finely chopped spinach
1 medium onion, peeled and roughly chopped
200 ml (⅓ pint) water
25 ml (1½ tbsp) butter
salt and pepper
oil for deep frying

Serves: 6
Preparation time: 10 minutes
Cooking time: 25 minutes

Put the whey, moong dal, spinach, onion and the water into a large pan. Cook for 15 minutes, then blend in a blender or food processor.

11

Strain the liquid and add the butter, then season with salt and pepper.

Cut half the soft cheese into long thin strips or very small squares. Wrap the remaining cheese in cling film and store in the refrigerator for up to 2 days. Heat the oil in a deep-fat fryer (kadai) and when hot, drop in the cheese, a few pieces at a time. Cook until golden brown, remove with a slotted spoon, then drain on absorbent kitchen paper. Continue in this way until all the cheese is fried. Add the fried cheese to the soup and serve hot.

VARIATION
If preferred, the soft cheese may be added to the soup uncooked.

CORN AND DAL SOUP
Moong dal aur makai soup

For this unusual, colourful and tasty soup, use one small can of creamed corn if fresh corn is not available. Serve with grated cheese.

Serves: 6
Preparation time: 15 minutes
Cooking time: 25 minutes

2 tender corn on the cob kernels, grated
15 ml (1 level tbsp) moong dal
1.1 litres (2 pints) water
15 ml (1 tbsp) butter
1 medium onion, peeled and roughly chopped
15 ml (1 tbsp) finely chopped celery
1 medium tomato, roughly chopped
15 ml (1 level tbsp) cornflour
40 g (1½ oz) finely chopped spinach
45 ml (3 tbsp) tomato ketchup
5 ml (1 tsp) lemon juice
salt and pepper

Put the corn with the moong dal and the water into a pan. Bring to the boil, then simmer for 15 minutes or until tender.

Melt the butter in a frying pan and fry the onion and celery for 1 minute. Add the cooked corn and its liquid with the chopped tomato. Mix the cornflour in a little water and add to the soup. Bring to the boil and boil for 10 minutes.

Add the spinach, tomato ketchup and lemon juice. Season with salt and pepper to taste and serve hot with grated cheese, if wished.

MULLIGATAWNY SOUP

This soup is a favourite in South India.

30 ml (2 level tbsp) coriander seeds
15 ml (1 level tbsp) cumin seeds
15 ml (1 level tbsp) aniseed (saunf)
1.25 ml (¼ level tsp) fenugreek seeds (methi)
2×2.5 cm (1 inch) cinnamon sticks
30 ml (2 tbsp) oil
2 medium onions, peeled and roughly chopped
2 carrots, peeled and roughly chopped
1 cm (½ inch) piece fresh ginger, peeled and finely chopped
4 garlic cloves, peeled and finely chopped
150 g (5 oz) masoor dal or toovar dal, washed
3 large tomatoes, roughly chopped
1.25 ml (¼ level tsp) turmeric powder
1 litre (1⅔ pints) water
200 ml (⅓ pint) thick coconut milk (page 116)
45 ml (3 tbsp) cooked rice
lemon juice, to taste
salt

Serves: 8
Preparation time: 20 minutes
Cooking time: 30 minutes

Dry roast the coriander seeds, cumin seeds, aniseed, fenugreek seeds and cinnamon sticks in a hot heavy-based pan or griddle (tawa) until they release their aroma. Grind into a powder in a small coffee grinder or with a mortar and pestle, then sieve.

Heat the oil in a pan, add the onions, carrots, ginger and garlic and fry for 2 minutes. Add the dal, tomatoes, ground roasted spices, turmeric powder and the water. Cover and cook for 15 minutes or until the vegetables are tender. Pour into a blender or food processor and blend, then strain.

Add the coconut milk, cooked rice and lemon juice to the soup. Season with salt and serve hot.

SPICED DAL SOUP

Masaledar dal ka showa

Serves: 4–6
Preparation time: 10 minutes
Cooking time: 1 hour

100 g (4 oz) chana dal
900 ml (1½ pints) water
5 ml (1 tsp) cumin seeds
10 ml (2 tsp) coriander seeds
5 ml (1 tsp) fenugreek seeds
3 dried red chillies
15 ml (1 tbsp) shredded coconut
30 ml (2 tbsp) ghee
225 g (8 oz) tomatoes, skinned and roughly chopped
2.5 ml (½ tsp) turmeric
15 ml (1 tbsp) tamarind water (optional page 118)
5 ml (1 tsp) salt
lemon slices and sprigs of coriander, to garnish

Wash the dal thoroughly in several changes of water. Put the dal into a pan with 600 ml (1 pint) of the water. Bring to the boil, cover and simmer until tender.

Grind the cumin, coriander, fenugreek, chillies and coconut in a small coffee or electric grinder or use a mortar and pestle.

Heat the ghee in a heavy-based frying pan or griddle (tawa), add the spice mixture and fry, stirring, for 30 seconds. Set aside.

Mash or liquidise the dal and transfer to a large saucepan. Stir in the tomatoes, spices, turmeric, tamarind juice, if using, salt and the remaining water.

Bring to the boil, then lower the heat, cover and simmer for about 20 minutes. Taste and adjust seasoning and turn into a warmed serving dish. Garnish with lemon slices and coriander sprigs and serve immediately.

VEGETABLE DISHES
AND CURRIES

The range of vegetable dishes prepared in India is the largest in the world. In fact, it's easy to see that with the wide range of spices available, combined with the large number of vegetables, the permutations for vegetable dishes are almost limitless. Remember, too, that the preparation varies from region to region and that within the region, it varies from household to household!

Vegetable dishes can be made with or without a sauce. Those containing thick hot spicy sauces or gravies are called curries. (A distinction needs to be made between ordinary vegetable curries and those made with the so-called curry powder. The latter is a proprietary brand of masala powder which is relatively bland to suit the palates of the average Westerner. Although curry powder is also used in India, most cooks prefer the taste and flavour of freshly ground masala.) Whether dry, or with a sauce, all vegetable dishes are eaten with Indian breads and rice.

MIXED VEGETABLES BHOPALI-STYLE
Bhopali sabji

The use of ghee will enhance the flavour of this delicately spiced vegetable dish.

Serves: 6
Preparation time: 20 minutes
Cooking time: 20 minutes

100 g (4 oz) potatoes, peeled and diced
100 g (4 oz) carrots, peeled and diced
100 g (4 oz) French beans, diced
100 g (4 oz) cauliflower, divided into small florets
100 g (4 oz) shelled green peas
75 ml (5 tbsp) oil or 45 ml (3 tbsp) ghee (page 113)
30 ml (2 level tbsp) cashew nuts (optional)
150 ml (¼ pint) water
45 ml (3 tbsp) milk
30 ml (2 tbsp) cream
2 pinches of sugar
salt

PASTE
8–10 garlic cloves, peeled
6 cloves
10 green chillies
seeds of 4 cardamoms
15 ml (1 level tbsp) coriander seeds
10 ml (2 level tsp) cumin seeds
2.5 cm (1 inch) piece fresh ginger, peeled
90 ml (6 tbsp) finely chopped fresh coriander leaves

Put all the vegetables into one pan with just enough water to cover and bring to the boil. Cover and simmer until just tender then drain and set aside.

Blend the ingredients for the paste in a blender or food processor with a little water.

Heat the oil or ghee in a large frying pan and fry the cashew nuts, if using, for 1 minute. Remove from the pan with a slotted spoon and set aside.

Add the paste to the pan and fry for 2–3 minutes. Add the vegetables and fry for 1 minute. Pour in the water and cook until the vegetables are soft.

Mix the milk and cream and add to the vegetables, stirring, then add the sugar and season with salt. Serve at once topped with the fried cashew nuts.

Herb Soup (see page 11)

BAKED CABBAGE
Bake bandhgobhi

This attractive dish can be made with cabbage or cauliflower.

1 medium cabbage, quartered
salt
100 g (4 oz) fresh or frozen shelled green peas
60 ml (4 tbsp) cream
30 ml (2 tbsp) cheese, grated

PASTE
1 medium onion, roughly chopped
100 ml (4 fl oz) water
2 medium tomatoes, roughly chopped
4 red chillies
2.5 cm (1 inch) stick cinnamon
3 cloves
1 cm (½ inch) piece fresh ginger, peeled
3 garlic cloves, peeled

SAUCE
30 ml (2 tbsp) butter
1 medium onion, peeled and finely chopped
1 bay leaf
200 ml (⅓ pint) water
salt
2.5 ml (½ level tsp) sugar (optional)

VEGETABLE
DISHES AND
CURRIES

Serves: 6
Preparation time: 20 minutes
Cooking time: 30 minutes

Heat the oven to very hot, 230°C/450°F/Gas mark 8.

Put the cabbage into a pan of boiling, salted water and cook for 10 minutes or until the cabbage is still slightly crunchy. Remove with a slotted spoon and keep warm. Boil the peas, simmer until just tender, then drain and set aside.

To make the paste: put the onion into a blender or food processor with the water. Add the remaining ingredients for the paste and blend until smooth.

To make the sauce: melt the butter in a heavy-based casserole. Add the onion and bay leaf and gently fry until the onion is soft. Add the paste mixture and continue frying for 3 minutes more. Pour in the water, season with salt and boil, uncovered, for 5 minutes. Remove from the heat, then stir in the sugar, if using.

Put the cabbage into a shallow serving dish. Cut out and remove any hard stem in the centre with a sharp knife. Pour over the sauce, then sprinkle over the peas. Pour over the cream and top with the cheese. Bake in the oven for 10–15 minutes or until golden brown and bubbling. Serve at once.

17

Spicy Cabbage (see page 20)

MIXED BEAN SPROUTS WITH FENUGREEK BALLS

Moong chana methi pakodi ke saath

Sprouted pulses and green masala combine deliciously with the flavour of fenugreek.

Serves: 6–8
Preparation time: 20 minutes
Cooking time: 30 minutes

175 g (6 oz) moong sprouts
175 g (6 oz) math sprouts
175 g (6 oz) chana sprouts
salt
30 ml (2 tbsp) oil plus oil for deep frying
400 ml (⅔ pint) thin coconut milk (page 116)

PASTE
40 g (1½ oz) fresh coriander leaves, finely chopped
7 green chillies
2.5 cm (1 inch) piece fresh ginger, peeled
7 garlic cloves, peeled
juice of 1 lemon
30 ml (2 tbsp) grated fresh coconut or flaked coconut

FENUGREEK BALLS
300 ml (½ pint) fenugreek leaves (methi bhaji), finely chopped
125 g (4 oz) wholemeal flour (gehun ka atta)
2.5 ml (½ level tsp) asafoetida powder
5 ml (1 level tsp) sugar
2.5 ml (½ level tsp) chilli powder
20 ml (4 tsp) hot oil

Put the moong, math and chana sprouts into a pan of boiling, salted water and boil for 15–20 minutes or until soft.

Drain and reserve the bean sprouts.

Blend the ingredients for the paste in a blender or food processor.

Heat the 30 ml (2 tbsp) oil in a saucepan over moderate heat and add the paste. Fry, stirring, for 3–4 minutes. Add the bean sprouts, coconut milk and season with salt. Cook over low heat for 5 minutes and keep hot.

Make the fenugreek balls: mix all the ingredients together including the 20 ml (4 tsp) hot oil and shape into walnut-sized balls.

Heat the oil for frying in a deep-fat fryer (kadai) and when hot, add the fenugreek balls in small batches. Cook until golden brown, remove with a slotted spoon and drain on absorbent kitchen paper. Continue in this way until all the balls have been cooked.

Just before serving, add the fenugreek balls to the pulse mixture, then serve.

SAVOURY CAKE BAKED IN COCONUT SAUCE

Idli naariyal ka doodh mein

A quick and tasty main dish, it is also a good choice for parties.

1 packet (200 g/7 oz) idli mix
15 ml (1 tbsp) ghee (page 113)
2.5 ml (½ level tsp) cumin seeds
2 curry leaves
2 green chillies, slit
5 ml (1 level tsp) plain flour (maida)
600 ml (1 pint) thin coconut milk (page 116)
salt
5 ml (1 tsp) lemon juice

Serves: 6
Preparation time: 15 minutes
Cooking time: 20 minutes

PASTE
1 medium onion, peeled
2 green chillies
2–3×2.5 cm (1 inch) pieces fresh ginger, peeled

Blend the ingredients for the paste in a blender or food processor with a little water.

Heat the oven to 200°C/400°F/Gas mark 6. Grease a 17.5 cm (7 inch) diameter ring mould tin and heat it. Prepare the idli mix as directed on the packet and pour it into the heated mould tin. Steam for 10 minutes.

Meanwhile, heat the ghee in a saucepan and fry the cumin seeds until they splutter. Add the curry leaves and green chillies and fry for 30 seconds more, then add the paste and plain flour and fry for 1 minute more. Add the coconut milk and season with salt. Boil for 5 minutes then add the lemon juice.

Invert the mould on to an ovenproof plate. Just before serving, pour the coconut sauce over the mould and bake in the oven for 10 minutes.

SPICY CABBAGE
Masala gobhi

This Punjabi-style dry cabbage dish is prepared with a slightly different masala mixture.

Serves: 6–8
Preparation time: 15 minutes
Cooking time: 20 minutes

75 ml (5 tbsp) oil
5 ml (1 level tsp) coriander seeds
30 ml (2 level tbsp) cumin seeds
5 ml (1 tsp) ajwain
1 kg (2¼ lb) cabbage, roughly chopped
3–4 large potatoes, peeled and roughly chopped
3–4 large onions, peeled and roughly chopped
10 small whole green chillies
50 g (2 oz) fresh ginger, peeled and sliced
30 ml (2 level tbsp) coriander powder
30 ml (2 level tbsp) cumin powder
15 ml (1 level tbsp) chilli powder
30 ml (2 level tbsp) amchur powder
1.25 ml (¼ level tsp) asafoetida powder
salt
30 ml (2 tbsp) finely chopped fresh coriander leaves

Heat the oil in a large frying pan and gently fry the coriander and cumin seeds with the ajwain for 30 seconds

Add the vegetables, chillies and ginger with the coriander, cumin, chilli, amchur and asafoetida powders. Season with salt and mix thoroughly. Cover and cook for about 15–20 minutes until the vegetables are soft. Sprinkle coriander leaves on top and serve.

STUFFED TOMATOES
Bhare hooey tamatar

Cabbage makes an excellent stuffing for tomatoes and provides a good contrast, both in colour and texture.

Serves: 6
Preparation time: 20 minutes
Cooking time: 10 minutes

salt
450 g (1 lb) cabbage, grated
2.5 ml (½ level tsp) turmeric powder
10 ml (2 level tsp) coriander-cumin seed powder (dhana-jira, page 113)
10 ml (2 level tsp) chilli powder
10 ml (2 level tsp) sugar
60 ml (4 tbsp) finely chopped fresh coriander leaves
700 g (1½ lb) medium tomatoes
45–60 ml (3–4 tbsp) oil

Sprinkle 5 ml (1 tsp) salt over the cabbage and set aside. After
10 minutes, squeeze out the water by pressing with the hands.

Add the turmeric, coriander-cumin and chilli powders, sugar and
salt to taste. Add the coriander leaves, reserving a few for garnish.
Make four slits in each tomato and gently open the tomatoes out so
that they can be stuffed. Fill them with the cabbage mixture.

Heat 45–60 ml (3–4 tbsp) oil in a large pan and arrange the
tomatoes in it. Cover and cook for 10 minutes until the tomatoes are
soft. Sprinkle with the reserved coriander leaves on top and serve.

MIXED VEGETABLES
Milijhuli sabji

So quick to prepare, this vegetable dish is ideal for a hurried snack; it is
also excellent for using up left-over boiled vegetables.

30 ml (2 tbsp) ghee (page 113)
2.5 ml (½ level tsp) cumin seeds
1 medium onion, peeled and sliced
1.25 ml (¼ level tsp) turmeric powder
4 garlic cloves, peeled and finely chopped
5 ml (1 level tsp) finely chopped fresh ginger
2 green chillies, finely chopped
30 ml (2 tbsp) finely chopped fresh coriander leaves
1 medium tomato, roughly chopped
200 ml (⅓ pint) water
175 g (6 oz) mixed boiled vegetables
2.5 ml (½ level tsp) garam masala (page 116)
salt

Serves: 6
Preparation time: 15 minutes
Cooking time: 10 minutes

Heat the ghee in a large pan and fry the cumin seeds until they splutter.
Add the onion, turmeric powder, garlic, ginger, green chillies and
coriander leaves and fry for 3–4 minutes.

Add the tomato and continue frying until the tomato softens, then
add the water, mixed boiled vegetables and garam masala. Season with
salt and serve at once.

SPICY POTATOES
Shahi aloo

Serves: 4–6
Preparation time: 15 minutes
Cooking time: 15 minutes

This spicy dish goes well with puris (page 60), plain parathas (page 66) and plain rice.

12 small round potatoes
oil or ghee (page 113) for deep frying, plus 45 ml (3 tbsp) oil or 30 ml
*   (2 tbsp) ghee*
1 large tomato, chopped
30 ml (2 tbsp) natural yogurt (dahi, page 114)
15 ml (1 tbsp) cashew nuts
15 ml (1 tbsp) raisins
100 ml (4 fl oz) water
2.5 ml (½ level tsp) sugar
salt
30 ml (2 tbsp) finely chopped fresh coriander leaves

PASTE
2.5 cm (1 inch) cinnamon stick
seeds of 2 cardamoms
3 cloves
6 black peppercorns
5 ml (1 level tsp) coriander seeds
2.5 ml (½ level tsp) cumin seeds
5 ml (1 level tsp) poppy seeds (khus-khus)
1 cm (½ inch) piece fresh ginger
3 garlic cloves, skinned

Prick the potatoes with a fork. Heat the oil or ghee in a deep-fat fryer (kadai) and when hot, add the potatoes. Cook until golden brown, remove with a slotted spoon and drain on absorbent kitchen paper.

Blend the ingredients for the paste in a blender or food processor with a little water.

Heat the 45 ml (3 tbsp) oil or 30 ml (2 tbsp) ghee in a large pan and fry the paste for 1–2 minutes. Add the tomato and yogurt and fry for 1 minute more, then add the cashew nuts and raisins and fry for 30 seconds.

Add the potatoes to the pan with the water and cook for 3–4 minutes. Add the sugar and salt to taste. Sprinkle coriander leaves on top and serve.

STUFFED POTATOES AND TOMATOES
Aloo aur tamatar ka bharva

Stuffed vegetables are very popular in India and most states have their own specialities. This dish uses the Maharashtrian style of masala, and goes very well with plain parathas (page 66).

Serves: 6–8
Preparation time: 20 minutes
Cooking time: 20 minutes

15 medium potatoes, scrubbed
10 medium tomatoes
90 ml (6 tbsp) oil
1 pinch of asafoetida powder (optional)
800 ml (1⅓ pints) water
45 ml (3 tbsp) finely chopped fresh coriander leaves

PASTE
30 ml (2 tbsp) oil
1 onion, peeled and sliced
½ dried coconut, grated or 45 ml (3 level tbsp) desiccated or flaked coconut
10 garlic cloves, peeled
45 ml (3 level tbsp) coriander seeds
45 ml (3 level tbsp) aniseed (saunf)
30 ml (2 level tbsp) poppy seeds (khus-khus)
10 black peppercorns
45 ml (3 level tbsp) chilli powder
5 ml (1 level tsp) turmeric powder
60 ml (4 tbsp) finely chopped coriander leaves

To make the paste: heat the oil in a frying pan and gently fry the onion, coconut, garlic, coriander seeds, aniseed, poppy seeds and peppercorns for 2 minutes.

Blend the mixture into a paste in a blender or food processor with a little water, then add the chilli and turmeric powders and coriander leaves. Make four slits in the potatoes and the tomatoes and stuff them with the paste.

Heat the 90 ml (6 tbsp) oil in a large pan and add the potatoes and tomatoes, asafoetida, if using, and the water. Cover and cook over medium heat for 20 minutes or until the vegetables are soft. Sprinkle coriander leaves on top and serve at once.

SOFT CHEESE IN SPICY TOMATO SAUCE
Kadai paneer

This dish, which comes from North India, goes very well with parathas (page 60). If you wish, you can reduce the spices without unduly affecting the taste.

Serves: 6
Preparation time: 20 minutes
plus 30 minutes soaking
Cooking time: 20 minutes

250 g (9 oz) soft cheese (pressed paneer, page 114)
ghee for deep frying (page 113) plus 45 ml (3 tbsp) ghee
3 medium onions, peeled and finely chopped
6 garlic cloves, peeled
1 cm (½ inch) piece fresh ginger, peeled
10 ml (2 level tsp) roasted cumin seed powder (page 118)
1.25 ml (¼ level tsp) turmeric powder
5 ml (1 level tsp) chilli powder
5 ml (1 level tsp) garam masala (page 116)
1 kg (2¼ lb) red tomatoes, skinned and roughly chopped
1 green pepper, seeded and sliced
salt

Cut the soft cheese into 2.5–5 cm (1–2 inch) wide strips.

Heat the ghee in a deep-fat fryer (kadai) and when hot, add the cheese strips in small batches.

Deep-fry lightly for 1–2 minutes, remove with a slotted spoon and put into tepid water for 30 minutes so that they become spongy.

Heat the 45 ml (3 tbsp) ghee in a frying pan and gently fry the onions until golden. Put the garlic and ginger into a blender or food processor and blend to a paste with a little water. Add the paste to the onions and fry for 30 seconds.

Add the cumin seed, turmeric, chilli powders and garam masala and fry again for 1 minute. Add the tomatoes and green pepper, cover and cook for 6–7 minutes.

Add the cheese strips to the pan with salt to taste, and cook for 2–3 minutes. Serve at once.

MIXED VEGETABLES SOUTH INDIAN-STYLE
◀ *Malabari sabji* ▶

This recipe from Kerala, the land of coconuts, naturally uses coconut to give the dish its distinctive aroma.

flesh of ½ coconut, grated or 25 g (1 oz) creamed coconut
60 ml (4 tbsp) water plus 400 ml (⅔ pint)
100 g (4 oz) French beans, diced
100 g (4 oz) carrots, peeled and diced
1 medium potato, peeled and diced
100 g (4 oz) cauliflower, divided into small florets
100 g (4 oz) shelled green peas
1 medium onion, peeled and roughly chopped
2 curry leaves
1.25 ml (¼ level tsp) turmeric powder
1 medium tomato, roughly chopped
2.5 ml (½ tsp) lemon juice
salt

PASTE
flesh of ½ coconut, grated or 25 g (1 oz) flaked or desiccated coconut
3–4 curry leaves
15 ml (1 level tbsp) rice
2 green chillies
6 garlic cloves, peeled
2.5 cm (1 inch) stick cinnamon
3 cloves
4 black peppercorns
3 red chillies

Serves: 6
Preparation time: 20 minutes
Cooking time: 25 minutes

To make the paste: mix the coconut, curry leaves and rice in a small pan. Stir constantly over a low heat until the mixture is light pink in colour. Add the green chillies, garlic, cinnamon, cloves, peppercorns and red chillies. Blend in a blender or food processor to a paste with a little water.

First make a thick coconut milk with the coconut and 60 ml (4 tbsp) water, then mix the remaining water to make a thin coconut milk (see page 116). Add the paste to the coconut milk and mix well.

Put all the vegetables, except the onion, into a pan and add the thin coconut milk. Add the onion, curry leaves and turmeric powder and cook until the vegetables are soft. Add the thick coconut milk and paste mixture with the chopped tomato. Boil for a further 2–3 minutes. Add the lemon juice and season with salt. Serve at once.

SPICY CORN
Masala makai

Dip the corncobs in the gravy from time to time whilst eating. The spicy gravy and tender corn make a mouth-watering combination.

Serves: 6
Preparation time: 20 minutes
Cooking time: 40 minutes

6 tender corn on the cobs, fresh or frozen
salt
3 large tomatoes, roughly chopped
600 ml (1 pint) water
30 ml (2 tbsp) ghee (page 113)
30 ml (2 tbsp) natural yogurt (dahi, page 114)
15 ml (1 tbsp) cream
2.5 ml (½ level tsp) sugar (optional)

PASTE
1 small onion, peeled and roughly chopped
6 garlic cloves, peeled
5 ml (1 level tbsp) coriander seeds
10 ml (2 level tsp) cumin seeds
2.5 cm (1 inch) piece fresh ginger, peeled
4 red chillies
2 green chillies
2×2.5 cm (1 inch) cinnamon sticks
2 cloves
seeds of 2 cardamoms

Cook the corn in a pan of boiling, salted water for 15 minutes or until tender.

Meanwhile, put the tomatoes into a pan with half the water and simmer, uncovered, for 15 minutes. Drain the corn and set aside to cool.

Purée the tomatoes in a blender or food processor, then sieve.

Blend the ingredients for the paste in a blender or food processor with a little water. Heat the ghee in a flameproof casserole and fry the paste for 4 minutes.

Cut each corn on the cob into four pieces and add to the paste with the tomato, the remaining water, and the yogurt. Season with salt and simmer gently for 15 minutes.

Just before serving, stir in the cream and sugar, if using, and mix well.

PAHADI POTATOES
Pahadi aloo sabji

This spicy vegetable is an excellent dish to serve on cold days.

30 ml (2 tbsp) ghee (page 113)
5 ml (1 level tsp) cumin seeds
2×1 cm (½ inch) cinnamon sticks
2 cloves
1 kg (2¼ lb) potatoes, unpeeled and sliced
salt
150 ml (¼ pint) natural yogurt (dahi, page 114)
100 ml (4 fl oz) milk
1 large tomato, skinned and roughly chopped
100 ml (4 fl oz) water
15 ml (1 tbsp) cream (optional)
2.5 ml (½ level tsp) sugar (optional)

Serves: 6
Preparation time: 20 minutes
Cooking time: 20 minutes

PASTE
10 ml (2 tsp) oil
1 large onion, peeled and sliced
30 ml (2 tbsp) grated fresh or flaked coconut
5 ml (1 level tsp) aniseed (saunf)
2.5 cm (1 inch) piece fresh ginger, peeled
6 red chillies
6 garlic cloves
2.5 ml (½ level tsp) black peppercorns
2.5 ml (½ level tsp) nigella seeds (kalonji)

To make the paste: heat the oil in a frying pan and fry all the
ingredients for 2–3 minutes. Put into a blender or food processor and
blend to a smooth paste with a little water.

Heat the ghee in a large pan and fry the cumin seeds until they
splutter. Add the cinnamon and cloves and fry for 30 seconds more.
Add the potatoes and season with salt. Cover and cook until they
become soft.

Mix the yogurt, milk, paste and tomato with the water in a separate
bowl. Add to the vegetables and cook for 1 minute. Taste and add the
cream and sugar if you find the taste too spicy. Serve at once.

PATIALA-STYLE MIXED VEGETABLES
Patiala sabji

Vegetables prepared in this way are mildly spicy and make an excellent accompaniment for a hotter dish.

Serves: 6
Preparation time: 10 minutes
Cooking time: 20 minutes

175 g (6 oz) cauliflower, divided into florets
100 g (4 oz) carrots, peeled and cubed
100 g (4 oz) green pepper, seeded and cubed
150 g (5 oz) shelled green peas
45 ml (3 tbsp) ghee (page 113)
1 medium onion, peeled and finely chopped
75 ml (5 tbsp) water
1.25 ml (¼ level tsp) turmeric powder
1 green chilli, finely chopped
200 ml (⅓ pint) milk
2.5 ml (½ level tsp) sugar
2.5 ml (½ level tsp) cinnamon powder
salt
5 ml (1 level tsp) cornflour
15 ml (1 tbsp) finely chopped fresh coriander leaves

PASTE
3 garlic cloves, peeled
1 cm (½ inch) piece fresh ginger, peeled

Blend the ingredients for the paste in a blender or food processor with a little water.

Put all the vegetables except the onion into one pan with just enough water to cover and bring to the boil. Simmer until just tender, then drain and set aside.

Heat the ghee in a saucepan and gently fry the onion for 1 minute.

Mix the paste in 30 ml (2 tbsp) of the water and add to the onions with the turmeric powder and cook until the onions are soft. Add the vegetables, green chilli, milk, sugar and cinnamon powder. Season with salt.

Mix the cornflour in the remaining water and add to the mixture. Cook for 2–3 minutes, then sprinkle coriander leaves on top and serve at once.

ROYAL CAULIFLOWER
Shahi phoulgobhi

The large unbroken cauliflower with contrasting green peas and
colourful spices makes an attractive vegetable for special occasions.

1 large cauliflower
225 g (8 oz) shelled green peas
45 ml (3 tbsp) ghee (page 113)
1 medium onion, peeled and sliced
2 cardamoms
2 cloves
2 bay leaves
2.5 ml (½ level tsp) sugar
30 ml (2 tbsp) tomato purée
200 ml (⅓ pint) natural yogurt (dahi, page 114)
300 ml (½ pint) water
salt
45 ml (3 tbsp) finely chopped fresh coriander leaves

PASTE
2 cardamoms
3 cloves
10 ml (2 level tsp) coriander seeds
2.5 ml (½ level tsp) cumin seeds
1 bay leaf
6 garlic cloves, peeled
2.5 cm (1 inch) piece fresh ginger, peeled
2.5 cm (1 inch) cinnamon stick
2.5 ml (½ level tsp) turmeric powder
1 small onion
15 ml (1 tbsp) chopped cashew nuts
5 ml (1 level tsp) chilli powder

Serves: 6
Preparation time: 15 minutes
Cooking time: 30 minutes

Blend the ingredients for the paste in a blender or food processor with
a little water. Parboil the whole cauliflower for 6 minutes, then drain
and set aside. Boil the peas, simmer until just tender, then drain.

Heat the ghee in a large pan and gently fry the onion until golden.
Add the cardamoms, cloves, bay leaves and sugar and fry for
2–3 minutes. Add the paste and fry for 3–4 minutes or until the ghee
rises to the top. Add the tomato purée and yogurt and fry for
2–3 minutes more, then add the peas and the water. Lower the
cauliflower into the pan and season with salt. Simmer for 2–3 minutes.

Arrange the cauliflower in a serving dish. Pour the sauce on top,
garnish with coriander leaves and serve at once.

PUMPKIN AND POTATOES

Aloo pethe ka saag

Serves: 6–8
Preparation time: 15 minutes
Cooking time: 15 minutes

Serve this popular and tasty vegetable dish, prepared in the Marwari style, with urad dal puris (page 64).

45 ml (3 tbsp) ghee (page 113)
2 bay leaves
2×1 cm (½ inch) cinnamon sticks
2 cloves
seeds of 2 cardamoms
5 ml (1 level tsp) nigella seeds (kalonji)
2.5 ml (½ level tsp) mustard seeds
2.5 ml (½ level tsp) fenugreek seeds
30 ml (2 tbsp) natural yogurt (dahi, page 114)
1.25 ml (¼ level tsp) asafoetida powder
5 ml (1 level tsp) chilli powder
10 ml (2 level tsp) coriander-cumin seed powder (dhana-jira, page 113)
2.5 ml (½ level tsp) turmeric powder
1 medium tomato, roughly chopped
450 g (1 lb) potatoes, peeled and roughly chopped
450 g (1 lb) red pumpkin (pethe), peeled and roughly chopped
100 ml (4 fl oz) water
5 ml (1 tsp) amchur powder or lemon juice
2.5 ml (½ level tsp) sugar
salt

Heat the ghee in a large pan and fry the bay leaves, cinnamon, cloves, cardamoms, nigella, mustard and fenugreek seeds until the seeds splutter.

Add the yogurt, asafoetida, chilli, coriander-cumin seed and turmeric powders and fry for 2–3 minutes. Add the tomato and fry for 1 minute more, then add the potatoes, pumpkin and the water. Cover and cook on a medium heat for 10–12 minutes or until the vegetables are tender.

Add the amchur powder or lemon juice and sugar and season with salt.

PEA KOFTA AND POTATO CURRY
Mutter kofta aloo ke saath

Serve this curry with puris (page 60), parathas (page 60) or plain rice (page 50).

Serves 6–8
Preparation time: 25 minutes
Cooking time: 30 minutes

2 medium potatoes, peeled
225 g (8 oz) shelled green peas
5 ml (1 level tsp) poppy seeds (khus-khus)
2 green chillies, ground or finely chopped
30 ml (2 level tbsp) gram flour (besan)
salt
oil for deep frying
30 ml (2 tbsp) ghee (page 113)
1 medium onion, peeled and grated
45 ml (3 tbsp) tomato purée
200 ml (⅓ pint) water
2.5 ml (½ level tsp) sugar

PASTE
6 red chillies
5 ml (1 level tsp) cumin seeds
1.25 ml (¼ level tsp) turmeric powder
5 ml (1 level tsp) garam masala (page 116)
1 cm (½ inch) piece fresh ginger, peeled
4 garlic cloves, peeled

Blend the ingredients for the paste in a blender or food processor with a little water.

Boil the potatoes, drain and set aside to cool, then cut into large pieces. Boil the peas, simmer until just tender, then drain, cool and mash.

To make the koftas: add the poppy seeds to the peas with the green chillies and gram flour and season with salt. Mix thoroughly and shape into small balls.

Heat the oil in a deep-fat fryer (kadai) and when hot, add the balls in small batches. Cook until golden brown, remove with a slotted spoon, then drain on absorbent kitchen paper. Continue in this way until all the balls have been cooked. To make the curry: heat the ghee in a frying pan and gently fry the onion until golden. Add the paste and fry for 3–4 minutes more. Add the tomato purée and fry for 1 minute more. Add the water, sugar and season with salt. Add the potatoes and cook for 3–4 minutes.

Just before serving, add the koftas, give one boil and serve.

VEGETABLE
DISHES AND
CURRIES

Serves: 6
Preparation time: 15 minutes
Cooking time: 25 minutes

BAKED SPICY VEGETABLES ON TOAST
Bake paaon bhaji ◄

This is a modified version of the highly popular dish in several Indian cities where it is sold on the roadside by street vendors with stoves on handcarts. They cook the spicy mixed vegetables on the spot on a griddle called a tawa and serve them spread over thick pieces of buttered bread. In this variation, the vegetables are grilled.

60 ml (4 tbsp) butter
2 medium onions, peeled and finely chopped
4 medium tomatoes, finely chopped
20 ml (4 level tsp) paaon bhaji masala (page 117)
5 ml (1 level tsp) chilli powder
1.25 ml (¼ level tsp) turmeric powder
30 ml (2 tbsp) finely chopped fresh coriander leaves
30 ml (2 tbsp) finely chopped green chillies
250 g (9 oz) mixed boiled vegetables
2 medium potatoes, boiled and roughly chopped
salt
6 slices of toast
45–60 ml (3–4 tbsp) cream
chilli powder to taste
grated cheese (optional)

Melt the butter in a heavy-based frying pan or griddle (tawa) and fry the onions until slightly brown in colour. Add the tomatoes, paaon bhaji masala, chilli powder, turmeric powder, coriander leaves and green chillies and fry for 4–5 minutes. Add the mixed vegetables and potatoes. Season with salt and sprinkle in a little water. Continue cooking for 2–3 minutes.

Spoon a little vegetable mixture on to each slice of toast, spread a little cream on top and dust with chilli powder to taste. If wished, sprinkle with a little grated cheese. Put the toast under a hot grill until the topping is hot. Serve at once.

Alternatively, put the vegetable mixture in a large ovenproof dish, spread the cream on top, sprinkle with cheese and bake in a preheated 200°C/400°F/Gas mark 6 oven for 15 minutes or until brown. Surround with slices of toast. Serve at once.

Opposite: Soft Cheese in Spicy Tomato Sauce (see page 24)
Overleaf: Spicy Potatoes (see page 22)

SOFT CHEESE KOFTAS IN SPINACH SAUCE

Paneer kofta palak ki kari mein

Kofta curries are very popular in India but the spinach sauce used in this dish makes it stand out from other kofta curries.

250 g (9 oz) finely chopped spinach
100 ml (4 fl oz) water
30 ml (2 tbsp) ghee (page 113)
150 ml (¼ pint) natural yogurt (dahi, page 114)
2.5 ml (½ level tsp) sugar
salt

Serves: 6
Preparation time: 15 minutes
Cooking time: 30 minutes

PASTE
15 ml (1 tbsp) grated fresh or flaked coconut
15 ml (1 tbsp) chopped cashew nuts
15 ml (1 level tbsp) poppy seeds (khus-khus)
4 garlic cloves, skinned
4–5 green chillies
2.5 cm (1 inch) piece fresh ginger, peeled
5 ml (1 level tsp) aniseed (saunf)

KOFTAS
175 g (6 oz) soft cheese (paneer, page 114)
60 ml (4 level tbsp) plain flour (maida)
30 ml (2 tbsp) finely chopped fresh coriander leaves
2 green chillies, finely chopped
1 pinch of bicarbonate of soda
salt
oil for deep frying

To make the koftas: Mix all the ingredients except the oil and shape into small balls. Heat the oil in a deep-fat fryer (kadai) and when hot, add the balls in small batches.

Cook until golden brown, remove with a slotted spoon, then drain on absorbent kitchen paper. Continue until all the balls are cooked.

Blend all the ingredients for the paste in a blender or food processor.

Put the spinach into a pan with the water. Bring to the boil, then simmer for 5–10 minutes until the leaves are soft. Drain thoroughly, then purée in a blender or food processor.

Heat the ghee in a large pan and fry the paste for 3–4 minutes. Add the yogurt and fry for 1 minute more, then add the spinach purée and sugar. Season with salt and boil for 3–4 minutes.

Just before serving, add the koftas and bring back to the boil. Serve.

Opposite: Chana Dal with Savoury Pakvans (see page 41)
Previous page: TOP *Baked Cabbage (see page 17)*
BOTTOM *Soft Cheese Koftas in Spinach Sauce (above)*

CHICK PEAS STEWED WITH TOMATOES
Chhole

Serves: 4
Preparation time: 15 minutes
plus overnight soaking
and 2–3 hours boiling
Cooking time: 20 minutes

Serve with any rice dish (pages 48–59) and natural yogurt, for a tasty, nutritious supper.

225 g (8 oz) white chick peas (kabuli chane)
4 garlic cloves, skinned and crushed
60 ml (4 tbsp) ghee or vegetable oil
2 medium onions, skinned and finely chopped
2 small green chillies, seeded and finely chopped
5 ml (1 level tsp) turmeric powder
5 ml (1 level tsp) paprika
15 ml (1 level tbsp) ground cumin
15 ml (1 level tbsp) ground coriander
5 ml (1 tsp) garam masala (page 116)
4 tomatoes, roughly chopped
30 ml (2 tbsp) chopped fresh coriander
15 ml (1 tbsp) chopped fresh mint
salt and pepper
chopped fresh mint to garnish

Wash the dried peas in several changes of water. Place in a large bowl, cover with plenty of fresh cold water and leave to soak overnight.

The next day, drain the chick peas and place in a large saucepan with half the garlic. Cover with plenty of water, bring to the boil, cover and simmer for 2–3 hours until tender. Drain well and set aside.

Heat the ghee in a heavy-based saucepan, add the remaining garlic and the chopped onions and fry gently for about 5 minutes until soft and lightly coloured. Add the chillies, turmeric, paprika, cumin, coriander and garam masala and fry, stirring, for a further 1–2 minutes.

Add the chopped tomatoes, coriander and mint and cook, stirring, for 5–10 minutes until the tomatoes turn to a purée.

Add the cooked chick peas and stir well. Simmer gently for another 5 minutes, or until the chick peas are heated through. Add salt and pepper to taste, then turn into a warmed serving dish. Serve hot with chopped mint.

PEA AND MUSHROOM CURRY
Shabnam kari

For those who do not like too hot a dish, this vegetable curry is only moderately spiced.

Serves: 6
Preparation time: 15 minutes
Cooking time: 15 minutes

100 g (4 oz) shelled green peas
30 ml (2 tbsp) ghee (page 113)
1 medium onion, peeled and finely chopped
2 cloves, peeled
15 ml (1 tbsp) raisins
100 g (4 oz) canned mushrooms, drained and sliced
45 ml (3 tbsp) cream
60 ml (4 tbsp) natural yogurt (dahi, page 114)
100 ml (4 fl oz) water
salt

PASTE
5 cloves
2.5 cm (1 inch) piece fresh ginger, peeled
30 ml (2 tbsp) chopped cashew nuts
30 ml (2 level tbsp) poppy seeds (khus-khus)
seeds of 2 cardamoms
6 green chillies

Blend the ingredients for the paste in a blender or food processor with a little water. Boil the peas, simmer until just tender, then drain and set aside.

Heat the ghee in a large pan and gently fry the onion until golden. Add the cloves and fry for 30 seconds more. Add the paste and raisins and fry for 2–3 minutes more, then add the peas, mushrooms, cream, yogurt and water. Season with salt and cook for 5 minutes. Serve at once.

QUICK POTATO CURRY
Jhatpat aloo kari

Serves: 4
Preparation time: 10 minutes
Cooking time: 15 minutes

A curry for those in a hurry. If you like, you can add some green peas and cut each potato in half.

2 medium tomatoes
1 medium onion, peeled and finely chopped
5 ml (1 tsp) finely chopped ginger
5 ml (1 tsp) finely chopped garlic
5 ml (1 level tsp) chilli powder
30 ml (2 tbsp) butter
2×1 cm (½ inch) cinnamon sticks
2 cloves
seeds of 2 cardamoms
10–12 round small potatoes, boiled and skinned
60 ml (4 tbsp) cream
salt
2.5 ml (½ level tsp) sugar (optional)

Put the tomatoes, onion, ginger, garlic and chilli powder in a blender and blend to a smooth paste.

Heat the butter in a large pan and gently fry the cinnamon, cloves and cardamoms for a few seconds. Add the tomato paste and fry for 2–3 minutes more, then add the potatoes and cream. Season and cook for 5–6 minutes. Add the sugar if necessary. Serve at once.

SCRAMBLED SOFT CHEESE
Paneer bhurji

Serves: 4
Preparation time: 10 minutes
Cooking time: 10 minutes

In this dish, soft cheese is cooked like a dry vegetable.

30 ml (2 tbsp) oil
1 medium onion, peeled and finely chopped
2 green chillies, finely chopped
1 cm (½ inch piece) fresh ginger, peeled and finely chopped
2 medium tomatoes, finely chopped
1.25 ml (¼ level tsp) chilli powder
1.25 ml (¼ level tsp) turmeric powder
1.25 ml (¼ level tsp) garam masala (page 116)
225 g (8 oz) soft cheese (paneer, page 114), crumbled
salt
30 ml (2 tbsp) finely chopped fresh coriander leaves

Heat the oil in a frying pan and gently fry the onion for 1 minute. Add
the green chillies and ginger and fry for 1 minute more. Add the
tomatoes, chilli and turmeric powders and the garam masala and
continue cooking for 1 minute.

Add the soft cheese and stir in with salt to taste. Cook for
1–2 minutes and serve hot topped with coriander leaves.

FRIED AUBERGINES
Jhat-pat baingan sabji

This dish, based on the Gujarati style of cooking, makes use of gram
flour which introduces an unusual taste.

250 g (10 oz) aubergines (baingan), sliced crossways
salt
oil for deep frying plus 30 ml (2 tbsp)
2.5 ml (½ level tsp) mustard seeds
5 ml (1 level tsp) sesame seeds (til)
2.5 ml (½ level tsp) chilli powder
2.5 ml (½ level tsp) turmeric powder
5 ml (1 level tsp) gram flour (besan)
2.5 ml (½ level tsp) sugar
15 ml (1 tbsp) cashew nuts
5–6 raisins

Serves: 4–6
Preparation time: 5 minutes
Cooking time: 15 minutes

Put the aubergine slices into a colander and sprinkle with salt. Leave
for about 20 minutes to draw out the bitter juices. Rinse thoroughly
and pat dry with absorbent kitchen paper.

Heat the oil in a deep-fat fryer (kadai) and when hot, add the
aubergine slices in small batches. Deep-fry until crisp, remove with a
slotted spoon and drain on absorbent kitchen paper. Continue in this
way until all the aubergines have been cooked.

Heat the 30 ml (2 tbsp) of oil in a large pan and fry the mustard
seeds until they splutter. Add the sesame seeds, chilli powder, turmeric
powder, gram flour, sugar, cashew nuts and raisins and fry for
1 minute.

Add the aubergines to the pan with salt to taste and cook for
1–2 minutes. Serve at once.

CAULIFLOWER AND PEA CURRY
Phoolgobhi aur mutter ki kari

Serves: 6
Preparation time: 15 minutes
Cooking time: 20 minutes

A coconut-based curry that gives the vegetables a delicious nutty flavour.

100 g (4 oz) shelled green peas
45 ml (3 tbsp) ghee (page 113)
175 g (6 oz) cauliflower, divided into small florets
2 bay leaves
2 medium tomatoes, grated
10 ml (2 tsp) natural yogurt (dahi, page 114)
100 ml (4 fl oz) water
30 ml (2 tbsp) chopped cashew nuts
2.5 ml (½ level tsp) sugar
salt

PASTE
1 medium onion, peeled and roughly chopped
30 ml (2 tbsp) grated fresh or flaked coconut
5 garlic cloves, peeled
10 ml (2 level tsp) coriander seeds
5 ml (1 level tsp) cumin seeds
2×1 cm (½ inch) cinnamon sticks
3 cloves
seeds of 3 cardamoms
1 cm (½ inch) piece fresh ginger, peeled
10 ml (2 level tsp) poppy seeds (khus-khus)
6 red chillies

Blend the ingredients for the paste in a blender or food processor with a little water. Boil the peas, simmer until just tender, then drain and set aside.

Heat the ghee in a large pan, add the cauliflower and peas and gently fry for 6–7 minutes. Remove the vegetables and set aside.

In the same ghee, add the bay leaves and paste and fry for 2–3 minutes. Add the tomatoes and yogurt and fry for 2–3 minutes more, then add the fried cauliflower, green peas and the water and cook on a low heat for 5–7 minutes until the vegetables are soft. Add the cashew nuts and sugar and season with salt. Serve at once.

CASHEW NUT AND GREEN PEA CURRY
◢ *Kaju mutter kari* ◣

Serve this rich moglai-style vegetable with coriander rotis (page 65), parathas (page 60) or plain rice (page 50).

250 g (9 oz) small round potatoes, peeled
oil for deep frying plus 30 ml (2 tbsp)
100 g (4 oz) shelled green peas
50 ml (2 fl oz) natural yogurt (dahi, page 114)
250 g (9 oz) soft cheese (paneer, page 114)
6 green chillies, finely chopped
15 g (½ oz) cashew nuts, roughly chopped
salt
30 ml (2 tbsp) finely chopped fresh coriander leaves

PASTE
2.5 cm (1 inch) cinnamon stick
seeds of 2 cardamoms
1 large black cardamom
3 cloves
6 black peppercorns
2 Kashmiri red chillies
2.5 ml (½ level tsp) cumin seeds
2.5 ml (½ level tsp) coriander seeds
5 ml (1 level tsp) poppy seeds (khus-khus)
2.5 cm (1 inch) piece fresh ginger, peeled

Serves: 4–6
Preparation time: 20 minutes
Cooking time: 30 minutes

Heat the oven to 180°C/350°F/Gas mark 4. Prick the potatoes with a fork. Heat the oil for frying in a deep-fat fryer (kadai) and when hot, add the potatoes. Fry until cooked. Remove with a slotted spoon, then drain on absorbent kitchen paper and keep warm.

Boil the peas, simmer until just tender, then drain and set aside.

To make the paste: blend all the ingredients for the paste in a blender or food processor with a little water.

Heat the 30 ml (2 tbsp) oil and fry the paste for 2 minutes. Add the yogurt and fry for 2 minutes more.

Pour into a medium, deep baking dish. Add the potatoes, soft cheese, peas, two-thirds of the green chillies and the cashew nuts. Season with salt, cover and bake in the oven for 15 minutes. Garnish with the remaining green chillies and coriander leaves and serve at once.

DALS AND KADHIS

Dals (beans and pulses) form the main source of protein for the Indian vegetarian. Most vegetarian meals include dals, not only for their nutritional value, but also because they provide a tasty gravy dish.

Each region of the country has its own preference for dals and also its own way of cooking them. Generally speaking, however, toovar and urad are the most popular, although moong are considered much easier to digest (moong water, in which the dal have been soaked or cooked, is given to convalescents to drink). Dals considered hard to digest are cooked with a variety of spices (including the strongly flavoured asafoetida powder) which help them to be more easily digested.

Kadhis (gram flour fritters in a natural yogurt sauce) are popular in Gujarat, Rajasthan and Punjab. The natural yogurt imparts a slightly sour taste and makes them all the more interesting.

CHANA DAL WITH SAVOURY PAKVANS
Pakvan aur chana dal

This is a popular dish from Sind. The pakvans can also be eaten as a snack with chutney.

225 g (8 oz) chana dal
30 ml (2 tbsp) ghee (page 113) or oil
2 medium onions, peeled and finely chopped
5 ml (1 level tsp) cumin seeds
2 green chillies, slit
2.5 ml (½ level tsp) turmeric powder
salt
100 ml (4 fl oz) water
1 large tomato, finely chopped
30 ml (2 tbsp) finely chopped fresh coriander leaves
5 ml (1 level tsp) coriander-cumin seed powder (dhana-jira, page 113)
2.5 ml (½ level tsp) chilli powder
2 pinches of garam masala (page 116)

PAKVANS
225 g (8 oz) plain flour (maida)
125 g (4 oz) wholemeal flour (gehun ka atta)
5 ml (1 level tsp) cumin seeds
2.5 ml (½ level tsp) salt
oil for deep frying

Serves: 6–8
Preparation time: 20 minutes
plus 4 hours soaking
Cooking time: 40 minutes

Put the chana dal into a bowl, cover with cold water and leave to soak for 3–4 hours or if convenient overnight. Drain.

Mix all the ingredients for the pakvans, except the oil, and add enough water to make a stiff dough. Knead well. Divide the dough into 15 pieces. Roll out each piece into rounds of 10–12 cm (4–5 inches) diameter. Prick all over with a fork.

Heat the oil in a deep-fat fryer (kadai) and when hot, add the rounds in small batches. Deep-fry until golden brown, remove with a slotted spoon, then drain on absorbent kitchen paper. Continue in this way until all the pakvans are cooked. Heat the ghee in a saucepan and fry the onions, cumin seeds and chillies until the onions are light brown in colour. Add the chana dal and turmeric powder. Season with salt and add the water. Cover and cook on a slow heat for 15–20 minutes until soft. Add the tomato, coriander leaves, coriander-cumin seed powder and chilli powder and cook for 1 minute. Sprinkle the garam masala on top and serve hot with the pakvans. Serve with chopped onions and chutney.

Serves: 6–8
Preparation time: 15 minutes
Cooking time: 30 minutes

MIXED DAL
▬ *Panchkuti dal* ▬

This delightful combination of five pulses is moderately spiced.

15 ml (1 tbsp) urad dal
15 ml (1 tbsp) toovar dal
15 ml (1 tbsp) moong dal
15 ml (1 tbsp) chana dal
15 ml (1 tbsp) masoor dal
1.1 litres (2 pints) water
30 ml (2 tbsp) oil
5 ml (1 level tsp) mustard seeds
5 ml (1 level tsp) cumin seeds
2×1 cm (½ inch) cinnamon sticks
2 cloves
4 curry leaves
4 small red chillies
3 green chillies, finely chopped
10 ml (2 tsp) finely chopped fresh ginger
10 ml (2 tsp) finely chopped garlic
2 tomatoes, roughly chopped
2.5 ml (½ level tsp) garam masala (page 116)
30 ml (2 tbsp) finely chopped fresh coriander leaves
juice of 1 lemon
salt

Mix all the dals and put into a pan with the water. Bring to the boil, cover and simmer until soft. Drain and set aside.

Heat the oil in a saucepan and fry the mustard seeds, cumin seeds, cinnamon and cloves for 1 minute. Add the curry leaves, red chillies, green chillies, ginger and garlic and fry for 1 minute more. Add the tomatoes and garam masala and continue cooking for 1 minute. Add the dals, coriander and lemon juice and season with salt. Bring to the boil and boil for 1 minute. Serve at once.

MARWARI-STYLE KADHI
Marwari kadhi

This Rajasthani-style kadhi is a little spicier and more tart than other versions.

1 litre (1¾ pints) natural yogurt (dahi, page 114)
30 ml (2 level tbsp) gram flour (besan)
1.25 ml (¼ level tsp) turmeric powder
450 ml (¾ pint) water
salt

PAKODIS (optional)
125 g (4 oz) gram flour (besan)
30 ml (2 tbsp) finely chopped fresh coriander leaves
1.25 ml (¼ level tsp) turmeric powder
1.25 ml (¼ level tsp) bicarbonate of soda
5 ml (1 level tsp) cumin seeds
2 green chillies, finely chopped
salt
oil for deep frying

TEMPERING (vaghar)
45 ml (3 tbsp) oil
2×1 cm (½ inch) cinnamon sticks
2 cloves
2 red chillies
5 ml (1 level tsp) aniseed (saunf)
5 ml (1 level tsp) coriander seeds
5 ml (1 level tsp) cumin seeds
2.5 ml (½ level tsp) fenugreek seeds (methi)
10 ml (2 tsp) finely chopped fresh ginger
6 garlic cloves, peeled and finely chopped
4 curry leaves
5 ml (1 level tsp) chilli powder

Serves: 6–8
Preparation time: 20 minutes
Cooking time: 30 minutes

To make pakodis: mix all the ingredients for the pakodis except the oil and add a little water to make a thick batter. Heat the oil in a deep fat fryer (kadai) and when hot, drop in spoonfuls of the batter. Cook for 3–4 minutes until crisp and golden brown, remove with a slotted spoon, and drain on absorbent paper. Continue with rest of batter.

For the tempering: heat the oil in a saucepan and fry the tempering ingredients for at least 2 minutes.

Mix the yogurt, flour, turmeric powder and water. Beat and pour into the tempering. Season with salt and bring to the boil. Simmer for 10–15 minutes. Just before serving, add the pakodis.

43

MOONG DAL AND CAULIFLOWER MEDLEY
▬ *Dal aur phoulgobhi ragad* ▬

This style of dish combining dal with vegetables is traditional of cooking from South India.

Serves: 6–8
Preparation time: 10 minutes
Cooking time: 50 minutes

175 g (6 oz) moong dal with skin (moong dal chilke wali)
3.75 ml (¾ level tsp) mustard powder
1.25 ml (¼ level tsp) fenugreek seeds (methi)
15 ml (1 level tbsp) coriander seeds
15–30 ml (1–2 tbsp) tamarind paste
100 ml (4 fl oz) water plus 1.7 litres (3 pints)
2.5 ml (½ level tsp) turmeric powder plus 1 pinch
salt
60 ml (4 tbsp) oil
2 medium onions, peeled and thinly sliced
75 g (3 oz) cauliflower, divided into small florets
4–6 curry leaves
6 green chillies, halved
5 ml (1 level tsp) chilli powder
30–45 ml (2–3 tbsp) finely chopped fresh coriander leaves

Wipe the dals with a damp cloth, then roast them in a heavy-based pan or griddle (tawa) for 2–3 minutes. Dry roast the mustard powder, fenugreek and coriander seeds in a small heavy-based pan or griddle (tawa) for 30 seconds. Cool and grind in a small electric grinder or with a mortar and pestle.

Mix the tamarind paste in the 100 ml (4 fl oz) water. Pour the remaining water into a large pan and bring to the boil. Add the dals and the 2.5 ml (½ level tsp) turmeric powder. Add salt to taste and boil for 20–25 minutes until the dals are tender. Heat the oil in a saucepan and fry the onions for 1 minute, then add the cauliflower, curry leaves, green chillies and the pinch of turmeric powder and cook 15 minutes until the cauliflower is tender.

Add the dals, chilli powder, tamarind mixture and ground spices and cook for 10 minutes. Serve at once, garnished with coriander leaves.

VEGETABLE AND YOGURT KADHI
Dahi aur sabji

Serve this tasty version of the popular Gujarati kadhi with plain rice. Frozen vegetables can be substituted for fresh.

175 g (6 oz) carrots, peeled and diced
175 g (6 oz) French beans, finely chopped
175 g (6 oz) cauliflower, divided into small florets
175 g (6 oz) shelled green peas
450 ml (¾ pint) natural yogurt (dahi, page 114)
50 g (2 oz) gram flour (besan)
600 ml (1 pint) water
15 ml (1 tbsp) ghee (page 113)
5 ml (1 level tsp) mustard seeds
5 ml (1 level tsp) cumin seeds
1 medium onion, peeled and roughly chopped
5 ml (1 level tsp) chilli powder
1.25 ml (¼ level tsp) turmeric powder
1.25 ml (¼ level tsp) coriander-cumin seed powder
  (dhana-jira, page 113)
salt
30 ml (2 tbsp) finely chopped fresh coriander leaves

Serves: 6
Preparation time: 15 minutes
Cooking time: 30 minutes

Put all the vegetables into one pan with just enough water to cover and bring to the boil. Simmer until just tender, then drain and set aside.

Mix the yogurt and gram flour, add the water and beat well.

Heat the ghee in a saucepan and fry the mustard seeds and cumin seeds until they splutter. Add the onion and fry for 1 minute more. Add the chilli, turmeric and coriander-cumin seed powder and fry 30 seconds more. Add the yogurt mixture and boil for 10 minutes, stirring for the first 3 minutes. Add the vegetables and season with salt. Cook for 3 minutes then sprinkle coriander leaves on top and serve at once.

SPICY KOFTA
Kofta kadhi

DALS AND
KADHIS

Kadhis are traditionally made from gram flour and natural yogurt, but this tasty and unusual version omits the yogurt. Technically it is neither a true kadhi nor a curry but lies somewhere in between.

Serves: 6
Preparation time: 15 minutes
Cooking time: 30 minutes

2×2.5 cm (1 inch) cinnamon sticks
3 cloves
seeds of 2 cardamoms
2.5 ml (½ level tsp) chilli powder
30 ml (2 tbsp) ghee (page 113)
30 ml (2 level tbsp) gram flour (besan)
600 ml (1 pint) water
100 ml (4 fl oz) tamarind water (imli, page 118)
salt
30 ml (2 tbsp) cream

PASTE
30 ml (2 level tbsp) poppy seeds (khus-khus)
30 ml (2 tbsp) cashew nuts
6–8 garlic cloves, peeled
2.5 cm (1 inch) piece fresh ginger, peeled
4 green chillies
2 large tomatoes
15 ml (1 level tbsp) grated fresh or flaked coconut

KOFTAS
60 ml (4 tbsp) aubergines (brinjals), finely chopped
1 medium onion, peeled and finely chopped
100 g (4 oz) grated cabbage
2 green chillies, finely chopped
60 ml (4 level tbsp) gram flour (besan)
1.25 ml (¼ level tsp) baking powder
salt
oil for deep frying

Blend the ingredients for the paste in a blender or food processor with a little water. To make the koftas: mix all the ingredients except the oil with a little water and make a batter.

Heat the oil in a deep-fat fryer (kadai) and when hot, drop in teaspoonfuls of the batter and cook for about 3 minutes until golden brown. Remove with a slotted spoon, then drain on absorbent kitchen paper. Continue in this way until all the koftas are fried.

Grind the cinnamon, cloves, cardamoms and chilli powder in an electric grinder or with a mortar and pestle.

Heat the ghee in a large pan and fry the paste for 2 minutes. Add the

46

gram flour and fry for 1 minute more, then add the water, the tamarind water and ground spice mixture. Season with salt and boil for 5 minutes.

Just before serving, add the koftas and the cream and bring back to the boil. Serve at once.

TOOVAR DAL WITH TOMATOES
Saambhar

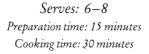

This spicy vegetable dal is cooked in the South Indian style.

350 g (12 oz) toovar dal
1 litre (1⅔ pints) water
200 g (7 oz) white pumpkin (lauki), cut into 4 cm (1½ inch) squares
6–8×5 cm (2 inch) pieces drumsticks (optional)
30 ml (2 tbsp) oil
2 medium onions, peeled and sliced
5 ml (1 level tsp) mustard seeds
5 ml (1 level tsp) fenugreek seeds (methi)
6–7 curry leaves
2 pinches of asafoetida powder
30 ml (2 level tbsp) saambhar powder (page 115)
30–45 ml (2–3 tbsp) tamarind paste
15 ml (1 tbsp) finely chopped fresh coriander leaves
salt
1 large or 2 medium tomatoes, quartered

Serves: 6–8
Preparation time: 15 minutes
Cooking time: 30 minutes

Wash the dal thoroughly in several changes of water. Put the dal into a pan with the water. Bring to the boil and cover and simmer until tender – do not overcook. Set aside.

Boil the pumpkin with the drumsticks, if using, drain and add to the cooked dal.

Heat the oil in a large pan and fry the onions, mustard seeds, fenugreek seeds and curry leaves for 2–3 minutes. Add the asafoetida and after a few seconds, add the cooked dal mixture, saambhar powder, tamarind paste and coriander leaves. Season with salt and boil for 5–7 minutes. Add the tomatoes and boil again for 2-3 minutes.

RICE DISHES

India has a very wide variety of regional rice dishes to offer, ranging from the pullavs and biryanis of the North to the dozens of bhaat dishes from the South. In fact, rice constitutes the staple diet of South Indians who use it with great imagination to produce scores of tasty dishes.

The method of cooking rice varies depending on the type of dish, and the final result itself will depend on the type of rice used, whether it was washed, whether soaked, the quantity of water used and so on. There are different schools of thought on many of these aspects and one learns best by experimenting.

TYPES OF RICE

Among the many varieties of long-grain rice available in the country, Basmati is king. Its tender and delicately perfumed grains make excellent pullavs and biryanis with a distinctive aroma. Like any other rice, this variety also improves with age and, usually, it is rice at least a year old that Indian cooks use. Another long-grained rice is the so-called Patna rice which is sold in the United Kingdom and other Western countries. Both Patna and Basmati can be used in pullavs and biryanis, although Basmati is preferred for the latter because in biryanis each cooked grain should be light, fluffy and separate. The medium- and short-grained varieties of rice tend to stick together and are more suitable for making khichadis and flours.

PREPARATION

Rice must be rinsed before cooking to remove the starchy powder left from the milling process. Cold water is used as hot water destroys the food value and also the aroma, and washing has to be done gently so that the grains do not break. After rinsing, some cooks soak the rice in water for 20–30 minutes so that the grains absorb a little water, thus reducing the tendency for individual grains to stick to each other. I personally do not find this necessary and have not specified it in any of the recipes. I have also not specified the use of salt (either in soaking or cooking) which some cooks add to the water to reduce the cooking time.

COOKING

Pullavs and biryanis should be cooked in plenty of water until 90 per cent cooked, and then drained.

For other rice dishes, use 1½–2 measures of water for every measure of rice, cover and cook until the water is absorbed. Cooking can also be done in a pressure cooker.

48

Vegetable and Yogurt Kadhi (see page 45)

AUBERGINE RICE
◀ *Vangi bhaat* ▶

A traditional rice dish in many parts of India, including Maharashtra, this version is based on the South Indian style of cooking.

Serves: 6–8
Preparation time: 30 minutes
Cooking time: 30 minutes

350 g (12 oz) Basmati rice
30 ml (2 tbsp) oil
2.5 ml (½ level tsp) mustard seeds
2.5 ml (½ level tsp) urad dal
2.5 ml (½ level tsp) chana dal
45 ml (3 tbsp) tamarind water (page 118)
1 large aubergine (brinjal), cut into long strips
a pinch of sugar
salt

DRY MASALA – use 10 ml (2 level tsp)
2×1 cm (½ inch) cinnamon sticks
4 cloves
seeds of 3 cardamoms
1.25 ml (¼ level tsp) asafoetida powder
20 ml (4 level tsp) coriander-cumin seed powder (dhana-jira, page 113)
6 red chillies
5 ml (1 level tsp) chana dal
2 black peppercorns

Roast all the ingredients for the dry masala in a heavy-based pan or griddle (tawa) until the spices release their aroma. Cool and crush in a coffee grinder or with a mortar and pestle. Store in an airtight container.

Put the rice into a sieve, wash under a cold running tap until the water runs clear. Boil the rice in a saucepan with plenty of water for about 15–20 minutes until it is cooked, each grain of the rice should be separate. Drain and cool.

Heat the oil in a large pan, add the mustard seeds, urad dal and chana dal and fry for 1 minute. Add the tamarind water and fry for 1 minute. Add the aubergine, 10 ml (2 level tsp) dry masala and the sugar. Season with salt and cook for 4–5 minutes or until the aubergine is soft. Add the rice and mix well. Serve hot.

TOP *Sultana Pullav (see page 53)*
BOTTOM *Sweet Rice (see page 58)*

PLAIN RICE
◀ *Uble chaval* ▶

Rice is a classic staple dish, and it is cooked here at its simplest.

250 g (9 oz) rice
600 ml (1 pint) water

Serves: 4
Preparation time: 5 minutes
plus 30 minutes soaking
Cooking time: 20 minutes

Put the rice into a sieve. Wash it thoroughly under a cold running tap until the water runs clear.

Drain in a sieve and let the rice stand for 1–2 minutes. Bring the water to the boil and add the rice.

Bring back to the boil, cover and cook for about 20 minutes or until the water is fully absorbed. Each grain of the boiled rice should be separate.

Fluff up the rice with a fork. Transfer the rice to a warmed serving dish. Serve hot.

VEGETABLE BIRYANI
◀ *Biryani* ▶

Rich pullavs containing ingredients like nuts and raisins are known as biryanis. Muslim in origin, they are traditionally non-vegetarian, but vegetarian versions such as this one are very tasty, and increasingly popular.

Serves: 8
Preparation time: 15 minutes
Cooking time: 1 hour

250 g (9 oz) Basmati rice
1.25 ml (¼ tsp) saffron
2.5 ml (½ tsp) warm water plus 15 ml (1 tbsp) hot water
salt
90 ml (6 tbsp) ghee (page 113)
2 medium onions, peeled and sliced
30 ml (2 tbsp) cashew nuts, broken into pieces
30 ml (2 tbsp) raisins
2 medium potatoes, peeled and diced
250 g (9 oz) cauliflower, divided into florets
3 medium carrots, scraped and cubed
2 green peppers, seeded, cored and cut into rings
3 medium tomatoes, finely chopped
175 g (6 oz) boiled green peas
15 ml (1 tbsp) finely chopped fresh coriander leaves
a little milk (optional)

PASTE
6 garlic cloves, peeled
2.5 cm (1 inch) piece fresh ginger, peeled
seeds of 3 cardamoms
5 green chillies
3 cloves
15 ml (1 level tbsp) poppy seeds (khus-khus)
2.5 cm (1 inch) cinnamon stick
2.5 ml (½ level tsp) turmeric powder
2.5 ml (½ level tsp) chilli powder
2 medium onions, peeled
6 mint leaves

Blend the ingredients for the paste in a blender or food processor with
a little water.

Put the rice into a sieve. Wash thoroughly under a cold running tap
until the water runs clear. Boil the rice in a saucepan with plenty of
water. When almost cooked, drain and cool. Put the saffron into a cup
with 2.5 ml (½ tsp) warm water and rub until it dissolves. Add to the
rice and season with salt.

Heat the oven to 230°C/450°F/Gas mark 8. Heat 60 ml (4 tbsp) ghee
in a pan and fry the onions until brown. Remove and set aside. In the
same ghee, add the cashew nuts and raisins and fry until the colour
changes. Remove and set aside. Add the paste and, if required, a little
more ghee and fry for 3–4 minutes.

Add the potatoes, cauliflower, carrots and green peppers to the pan.
Cover and cook for 10 minutes, then add the tomatoes, peas and the
15 ml (1 tbsp) hot water and continue cooking for 5–7 minutes. Add
the coriander leaves.

Spread 30 ml (2 tbsp) ghee in a bowl. Make alternate layers of rice
and vegetables beginning and ending with rice. If you like, sprinkle a
little milk on top. Cover and bake in the oven for 15–20 minutes. Turn
upside down into a serving dish, garnish with the fried onions, cashew
nuts and raisins and serve hot.

PEA AND CASHEW NUT PULLAV
Mutter kaju pullav

Serves: 6
Preparation time: 15 minutes
Cooking time: 15 minutes

Serve this substantial pullav with natural yogurt (see page 114)

175 g (6 oz) Basmati rice
45 ml (3 tbsp) ghee (page 113) or 60 ml (4 tbsp) oil
100 g (4 oz) cashew nuts
100 g (4 oz) shelled green peas
450 ml (¾ pint) water
salt
5 ml (1 level tsp) black cumin seeds (shah-jira)
15 ml (1 tbsp) freshly chopped fresh coriander leaves

PASTE
4 cloves
6 garlic cloves, peeled
8–10 green chillies
seeds of 2 cardamoms
10 ml (2 level tsp) coriander seeds
5 ml (1 level tsp) cumin seeds
60 ml (4 tbsp) finely chopped fresh coriander leaves
2.5 cm (1 inch) piece fresh ginger, peeled

Put the rice into a sieve. Wash thoroughly under a cold running tap until the water runs clear.

Blend the ingredients for the paste in a blender or food processor with a little water.

Heat half the ghee in a saucepan and fry the cashew nuts until they are light golden in colour. Remove the fried cashew nuts and set aside. In the same ghee, add the paste and fry for 1 minute. Add the peas and 100 ml (4 fl oz) of water and season with salt. Cook until the peas are tender.

Heat the remaining ghee in a saucepan and fry the black cumin seeds for 1 minute. Add the rice and cook for 1 minute. Add double the volume of water. Season with salt, cover and cook for 15 minutes. Uncover, add the pea mixture, mix well and cook for 1–2 minutes. Serve hot, topped with coriander leaves and the fried cashew nuts.

SULTANA PULLAV
Sultani pullav

Serve the cardamoms in the pullav to impart flavour.

250 g (9 oz) Basmati rice
750 ml (1¼ pints) water
3×2.5 cm (1 inch) cinnamon sticks
4 cloves
2 cardamoms, slightly opened
10 ml (2 level tsp) salt plus extra for seasoning
45 ml (3 tbsp) ghee (page 113)
2 onions, peeled and grated
2 large tomatoes, skinned and mashed
75 g (3 oz) shelled green peas
50 g (2 oz) cauliflower, divided into small florets
10 ml (2 level tsp) coriander-cumin seed powder (dhana-jira) (page 113)
10 ml (2 level tsp) chilli powder
10 ml (2 tsp) natural yogurt (dahi, page 114)
2.5 ml (½ level tsp) sugar
15 ml (tbsp) cream
25 g (1 oz) fried croûtons
150 ml (¼ pint) milk
1.25 ml (¼ tsp) rose essence or kewada (optional)
1.25 ml (¼ tsp) orange food colouring

PASTE
4 garlic cloves, peeled
1.25 cm (½ inch) piece fresh ginger, peeled
seeds of 2 cardamoms

RICE DISHES

Serves: 6
Preparation time: 15 minutes
plus 30 minutes soaking
Cooking time: 45 minutes

Put the rice into a sieve. Wash thoroughly under a cold running tap until the water runs clear.

Bring 600 ml (1 pint) of water to the boil and add the rice, cinnamon, cloves, cardamoms and salt. Bring back to the boil, cover and cook for about 20 minutes until the water is fully absorbed. Cool. Blend paste ingredients with a little water.

Heat the oven to 230°C/450°F/Gas mark 8. Heat 30 ml (2 tbsp) ghee in a saucepan and fry the onions until golden. Add the paste and fry for 1 minute, then add the mashed tomatoes, peas, cauliflower, coriander-cumin seed powder and chilli powder. Season with salt and add the remaining water and cook until the vegetables are soft. Add the yogurt, sugar and cream.

Put the remaining ghee into a large ovenproof bowl. Mix the croûtons with the rice and layer the rice and vegetables in the bowl. Mix the milk, essence and colouring and pour over the rice. Cover with kitchen foil, bake in the oven for 20–25 minutes. Serve hot.

RICE DISHES

CORN PULLAV
Makka ka chawal

Serves: 6
Preparation time: 15 minutes
Cooking time: 40 minutes

The colourful mixture of vegetables added to the rice makes this an attractive pullav to serve.

250 g (9 oz) Patna rice
60 ml (4 tbsp) ghee (page 113)
2×1 cm (½ inch) cinnamon sticks
2 cloves
175 g (6 oz) cooked corn
1 green pepper, seeded and roughly chopped
1 boiled carrot, diced
salt
200 ml (⅓ pint) natural yogurt (dahi, page 114)
30 ml (2 tbsp) cream
2.5 ml (½ level tsp) sugar
100 ml (4 fl oz) water

PASTE
1 medium onion, peeled and chopped
30 ml (2 tbsp) grated fresh or flaked coconut
5 garlic cloves, peeled
10 ml (2 level tsp) coriander seeds
5 ml (1 level tsp) cumin seeds
2×1 cm (½ inch) cinnamon sticks
2 cloves
seeds of 2 cardamoms
2.5 cm (1 inch) piece fresh ginger, peeled
10 ml (2 level tsp) poppy seeds (khus-khus)
6 red chillies

Put the rice into a sieve. Wash thoroughly under a cold running tap.

Boil the rice for 15–20 minutes until it is cooked. Drain and cool.

Heat the oven to 200°C/400°F/Gas mark 6. Blend the ingredients for the paste in a blender or food processor with a little water.

Heat half the ghee in a large pan and fry the cinnamon and cloves for 30 seconds. Add the cooked rice, corn, green pepper and carrot. Season with salt and continue frying for 1 minute.

Heat the remaining ghee in a saucepan and fry the paste for 3–4 minutes. Add the yogurt, cream and sugar. Season with salt, add the water and cook for 1 minute.

Spread half the rice mixture on a sheet of kitchen foil and spread the curry on top. Cover with the remaining rice mixture, fold over the kitchen foil and seal. Bake the parcel in the oven for about 20 minutes. Unwrap and serve hot.

CABBAGE RICE
Bandhgobhi chawal

This simple rice dish, without chillies but with the delicate flavour of butter, can be served with any kadhi or curry. If you like, sprinkle fried onions on top instead of cheese.

175 g (6 oz) Basmati rice
30 ml (2 tbsp) butter
1 medium onion, peeled and grated
75 g (3 oz) shredded cabbage
1 green pepper, seeded and sliced
2.5 ml (½ level tsp) pepper
salt
30 ml (2 tbsp) grated cheese

Serves: 4
Preparation time: 10 minutes
Cooking time: 20 minutes

Put the rice into a sieve. Wash thoroughly under a cold running tap until the water runs clear.

Boil the rice in a saucepan with plenty of water until it is cooked, each grain of the cooked rice should be separate. Drain and cool.

Heat the butter in a large pan and fry the onion for 2–3 minutes. Add the cabbage and green pepper and continue cooking for 2–3 minutes. Add the cooked rice, pepper and salt to taste. Sprinkle the cheese on top and serve hot.

PULSES PULLAV
Kathol pullav

Serves: 6–8
Preparation time: 15 minutes
plus 10 hours soaking
Cooking time: 20 minutes

Lentils and pulses have always been the main source of proteins for the Indian vegetarian population and, not surprisingly, they are used in a very wide variety of dishes. This pullav, containing three pulses, is protein-packed. Decorate with green pepper, cucumber slices and spring onions.

30 ml (2 tbsp) red kidney beans (rajma)
30 ml (2 tbsp) black-eyed beans (lobhia)
30 ml (2 tbsp) white chick peas (kabuli chane)
30 ml (2 tbsp) peanuts
700 g (1½ lbs) cooked Basmati rice
75 ml (5 tbsp) oil
salt
5 ml (1 level tsp) mustard seeds
2 medium onions, peeled and finely chopped
2 medium tomatoes, roughly chopped
5 ml (1 level tsp) chilli powder
5 ml (1 level tsp) garam masala (page 116)
50 g (2 oz) sprouted green chick peas (hare chane)
10 ml (2 tsp) lemon juice

Put the red kidney beans, black-eyed beans and white chick peas into a large bowl, cover with cold water and leave to soak overnight. Drain and boil rapidly together with the peanuts for 10 minutes then simmer until they are cooked. Drain.

Put the rice into a sieve. Wash thoroughly under a cold running tap until the water runs clear.

Heat 45 ml (3 tbsp) oil in a frying pan on a high heat, add the rice and cook for 2 minutes, then season with salt.

Heat the remaining oil in another frying pan, add the mustard seeds and heat until they splutter. Add the onions and tomatoes and fry for about 30 seconds. Add the chilli powder, garam masala, cooked pulses, sprouted green chick peas and lemon juice. Season with salt and cook for 3–4 minutes. Stir in the rice and serve at once.

SPICY RICE AND LENTILS
Masala khichadi

Khichadis are cooked mixtures of rice and different types of lentils; this is a highly spiced version. If you like, replace the potatoes with mixed vegetables such as cauliflower, carrots, French beans and green peas.

100 g (4 oz) long-grain rice
4–6 garlic cloves, peeled
2.5 cm (1 inch) piece fresh ginger, peeled
4 green chillies
30 ml (2 tbsp) ghee (page 113) or 45 ml (3 tbsp) oil
1 large onion, peeled and finely chopped
2 sticks cinnamon
2 cloves
2 bay leaves
2.5 cm (½ level tsp) turmeric powder
5 ml (1 level tsp) chilli powder
30 ml (2 level tbsp) moong dal
2 small potatoes, peeled and diced
salt

Serves: 4
Preparation time: 10 minutes
Cooking time: 25 minutes

Put the rice into a sieve and wash thoroughly under a cold running tap until the water runs clear.

Put the garlic, ginger and green chillies into a blender or food processor and blend to a paste with a little water.

Heat the ghee or oil in a deep pan or rice cooker and fry the onion for 1 minute. Add the cinnamon, cloves and bay leaves and fry for 30 seconds. Add the paste, turmeric powder and chilli powder and fry for 1 minute more, then add the rice and dal and fry for another minute.

Pour in warm water to cover the rice by about 5 cm (2 inches), then add the potatoes and season with salt. Cover and cook gently for about 15–20 minutes until the rice is tender and all the moisture has been absorbed. Serve hot.

SPROUTED MOONG KHICHADI
Masale dar moong ki khichadi

Serves: 6
Preparation time: 15 minutes
Cooking time: 20 minutes

This filling pullav is very easy to prepare.

175 g (6 oz) long-grain rice
45 ml (3 tbsp) oil
4 garlic cloves, crushed
100 g (4 oz) sprouted moong (page 119)
450 ml (¾ pint) warm water
60 ml (4 tbsp) grated fresh or flaked coconut
60 ml (4 tbsp) finely chopped fresh coriander leaves
10 ml (2 tsp) coriander-cumin seed powder (dhana-jira, page 113)
5 ml (1 level tsp) chilli powder
1.25 ml (¼ level tsp) turmeric powder
10 ml (2 level tsp) sugar
salt

Put the rice into a sieve. Wash thoroughly under a cold running tap until the water runs clear.

Heat the oil in a saucepan and fry the garlic for 30 seconds. Add the sprouted moong, rice, water, coconut, coriander leaves, coriander-cumin seed powder, chilli powder, turmeric powder and sugar. Season with salt, cover and cook for about 15–20 minutes until soft. Serve hot.

SWEET RICE
Meetha chawal

Meetha chawal is a traditional sweet rice eaten on festive occasions. This modified version enables the dish to be made in a surprisingly short time.

Serves: 6
Preparation time: 10 minutes
Cooking time: 10 minutes

350 g (12 oz) cooked Patna rice
100 g (4 oz) sugar
30 ml (2 tbsp) ghee (page 113)
2×1 cm (½ inch) cinnamon sticks
2 cloves
2 bay leaves
2 pinches of saffron
2.5 ml (½ tsp) warm water
a few blanched and sliced almonds and pistachios, to garnish

Mix the cooked rice and sugar.

Heat the ghee in a large pan and fry the cinnamon, cloves and bay leaves for 30 seconds, then add the rice.

Put the saffron into a cup with the water and rub until it dissolves. Add to the rice and cook until the sugar melts and the rice takes on a lovely orange colour.

Decorate with the almonds and pistachios and serve hot.

KHICHADI IN BENGALI-STYLE
Bengali khichadi

Use any vegetable combination of your choice in this spicy khichadi.

175 g (6 oz) long-grain rice
2.5 cm (1 inch) cinnamon stick
4 cloves
3 cardamoms
45 ml (3 tbsp) ghee (page 113)
1 medium onion, peeled and finely chopped plus 6–7 small onions,
   peeled (optional)
2 bay leaves
150 g (5 oz) masoor dal
8 small potatoes, peeled
10–12 French beans, cut into 2.5 cm (1 inch) pieces
50 g (2 oz) shelled green peas
2–3 green chillies, finely chopped
2.5 ml (½ level tsp) turmeric powder
4 garlic cloves, crushed
2.5 cm (1 inch) piece fresh ginger, peeled and grated
salt
1.7 litres (3 pints) hot water

Serves: 6–8
Preparation time: 15 minutes
Cooking time: 25 minutes

Put the rice into a sieve and wash thoroughly under a cold running tap until the water runs clear.

Crush the cinnamon, cloves and cardamoms lightly.

Heat 30 ml (2 tbsp) ghee in a large pan and fry the chopped onion, crushed spices and the bay leaves for 1 minute. Then add the rice, masoor dal, potatoes, whole small onions, if using, French beans, green peas, green chillies, turmeric powder, garlic and ginger. Season with salt and cook for 1 minute.

Add the water, cover and cook for about 20–25 minutes until the lentils are soft. Remove from heat, pour the remaining ghee on top and serve.

BREADS

The Indian sub-continent offers a large number of breads of different types but the basic ones are chapatis, parathas and puris and they are usually made with gehun ka atta (wholemeal flour), although they can be made with a mixture of wholemeal and plain if preferred.

Of these three, chapatis or rotis are the healthiest. They are made by dry-frying wholemeal dough on a tawa, which is a slightly concave cast-iron plate like a heavy griddle.

CHAPATIS

Because the dough used for making these breads is soft, a certain amount of dry flour has to be used for rolling. The dough ball is flattened by hand, then dipped in flour and, from time to time, flour is dusted on to the rolling surface. If the chapati sticks to the work surface during rolling, it should be lifted carefully and dipped once again in flour.

For cooking chapatis, the tawa must be preheated to prevent the chapatis from becoming hard and brittle. The chapati is added to the pan and dry roasted until bubbles and brown spots appear on the surface. Like other Indian breads, chapatis are cooked on both sides but the basic difference is that cooking is done without the addition of any fat. A well-cooked chapati should not only be light but also fluffy. Chapatis are served hot, generally after smearing a little ghee on top.

Cooked chapatis can also be stacked one on top of the other as they are being made and covered with a napkin to keep them hot. Naturally, the chapatis do deflate in the process, but the taste is not affected. Chapatis also freeze well; simply heat from frozen under a hot grill.

PARATHAS

Like chapatis, these are made from wholemeal dough, but they are prepared and cooked in a different manner. The addition of a little fat, and the method of folding the bread several times and rerolling after each folding process give parathas a distinctive character. Parathas are usually triangular shaped but can be square or circular.

Being shallow-fried, parathas are crisp on the outside and soft on the inside. They are cooked on a hot tawa until bubbles and spots appear on the surface. Like chapatis, they are cooked on both sides and the edges are pressed down to ensure proper cooking.

PURIS

Crisp and puffy, these breads are made from a slightly stiffer wholemeal dough which uses oil and much less water for binding the flour. After kneading, the dough is covered with a damp cloth and

allowed to rest for a while. The dough is then rolled out and deep-fried in a kadai, which is a pan very similar to the Chinese wok.

Although a deep-fat fryer can be used instead of the kadai, the concave shape of the kadai uses less oil. When the puri is ready to be turned, it is lifted with a slotted spoon and held along the sides of the pan allowing the oil to drain off without splashing. As the cooking oil should be very hot for frying puri, it is important to ensure that it does not splash. Adding the puris to the oil and turning them must be done very carefully.

LACHHI ROTI, BHATHURA AND NAANS
These breads are made with plain flour (maidu).

PLAIN PURIS
Puri

These plain puris for day-to-day use go very well with spicy vegetables, dals and kadhis.

250 g (9 oz) wholemeal flour (gehun ka atta)
15 ml (1 tbsp) ghee (see page 113) plus oil for deep frying

Makes 15–20 puris
Preparation time: 10 minutes
Cooking time: 30 minutes

Mix the flour and the 15 ml (1 tbsp) ghee and add enough water to make a semi-stiff dough. Knead the dough for 4–5 minutes. Divide into 15–20 portions. On a lightly floured surface roll out into rounds about 7.5 cm (3 inches) diameter.

Heat ghee or oil in a deep-fat fryer (kadai) and when hot, cook the puris a few at a time. When they puff up, turn on the other side with a slotted spoon and fry for a few seconds. Remove with a slotted spoon and place on absorbent kitchen paper to drain. Continue in this way until all the puris are cooked. Serve hot.

SPICY PURIS
Masala puri

Makes about 15 puris
Preparation time: 10 minutes
Cooking time: 20 minutes

Aniseed and nigella (onion) seeds impart a distinctive flavour to these tasty puris.

250 g (9 oz) wholemeal flour (gehun ka atta)
30 ml (2 tbsp) moong dal skins (optional)
5 ml (1 level tsp) aniseed (saunf)
2.5 ml (½ level tsp) nigella seeds (kalonji)
1.25 ml (¼ level tsp) asafoetida powder
15–20 ml (3–4 tsp) oil plus oil for deep frying
salt

PASTE
2.5 cm (1 inch) piece fresh ginger, peeled
4 green chillies

Blend the ginger and green chillies to a smooth paste in a blender or food processor with a little water.

Mix the flour, skins if using, aniseed, nigella seeds, asafoetida and the 15–20 ml (3–4 tsp) oil. Season with salt and add the ginger paste. Add enough water to make a semi-stiff dough. Roll out on a lightly floured surface into thin puris of 7.5 cm (3 inch) diameter.

Heat the remaining oil in a deep-fat fryer (kadai) and when hot, cook the puris a few at a time until golden brown. Remove with a slotted spoon and drain on absorbent kitchen paper. Serve hot.

SOFT CHEESE PUFFS
Paneer puris

For ease, ready-made bread dough can be used instead of the dough recipe given here.

250 g (9 oz) plain flour (maida)
10 g (⅓ oz) fresh yeast or 5 ml (1 level tsp) dried
2.5 ml (½ level tsp) sugar
100 ml (4 fl oz) warm water plus a little extra for the dough
2.5 ml (½ level tsp) salt
15 ml (1 tbsp) butter
ghee (page 113) for cooking
butter for spreading

STUFFING
175 g (6 oz) soft cheese (paneer, page 114)
1 medium onion, peeled and finely chopped
3 green chillies, chopped
15 ml (1 tbsp) finely chopped fresh coriander leaves
salt

Makes 10 puffs
Preparation time: 1 hour
Cooking time: 30 minutes

To make the stuffing: mix the soft cheese (paneer), onion, green chillies and coriander leaves and season with salt.

Sift the flour into a bowl and make a well in the centre. Add the yeast, sugar and the 100 ml (4 fl oz) water. Leave for a few minutes until the mixture bubbles. Add the salt and 15 ml (1 tbsp) butter and mix to a soft dough with a little warm water. Knead the dough for 6 minutes, then set aside under a wet cloth for 20 minutes or until double in size. Knead the dough for 1 minute, then divide into 10.

Roll each portion into a small puri of 7.5 cm (3 inch) diameter and fill with a little stuffing. Close and roll out again. Allow them to rest for 15 minutes.

Cook the puris on both sides in a heavy-based frying pan or griddle (tawa) lightly brushed with ghee. Serve hot with butter.

OVEN BAKING
These puffs can also be baked. Put into a very hot oven at 230°C/450°F/gas mark 8 for 15–20 minutes.

SPICY URAD DAL PURIS
◀ *Urad dal puri* ▶

Serves: 4
Preparation time: 20 minutes
plus 4 hours soaking
Cooking time: 30 minutes

These popular puris are served as a hot snack from roadside stalls in Rajasthan.

175 g (6 oz) urad dal
125 g (4 oz) plain flour (maida)
60 ml (4 tbsp) hot oil plus oil or ghee (page 113) for deep frying
2 pinches of salt
15 ml (1 level tbsp) coriander seeds
15 ml (1 level tbsp) cumin seeds
15 ml (1 level tbsp) aniseed (saunf)
8 black peppercorns
4 large or 8 small red chillies
salt

Put the dal into a bowl, cover with cold water and leave to soak for 4 hours. Drain and put into a blender or food processor with very little water and grind coarsely to a paste.

Mix the flour, 30 ml (2 tbsp) hot oil, the salt and enough water to make a stiff dough. Knead well and set aside for about 20 minutes.

Dry roast the coriander and cumin seeds with the aniseed, peppercorns and chillies in a heavy-based pan or griddle (tawa) for 1 minute. Grind into a powder in a small coffee grinder or with a mortar and pestle.

Put the remaining 30 ml (2 tbsp) oil in a large pan and fry the dal paste until light golden in colour. Cool, then add the powdered masala and salt to taste.

Divide the dough into 10 portions. Roll each out on a lightly floured surface into thin puris of 5–7.5 cm (2–3 inch) diameter. Put a little stuffing mixture on to each. Close the edges so as to enclose the stuffing completely. Roll out again into small puris.

Heat the oil for frying in a deep-fat fryer (kadai) and when hot, cook the puris a few at a time until golden brown. Remove with a slotted spoon and drain on absorbent kitchen paper. Serve hot with natural yogurt (dahi, page 114).

TOP *Layered Chapati Bake (see page 73)*
BOTTOM *Minty Corn and Vegetable Parathas (see page 66)*

CORIANDER ROTI
Hare dhaniya ki roti

Makes 8 rotis
Preparation time: 20 minutes
Cooking time: 30 minutes

Like most savoury-stuffed rotis and parathas, these are quite substantial and can be eaten on their own. The unusual method of rolling the dough out twice, which produces a decorative pattern for the stuffing, is optional, although it is not as complicated as it sounds. If you prefer, however, simply put the stuffing between two rotis and seal the edges before cooking.

250 g (9 oz) wholemeal flour (gehun ka atta)
10 ml (2 tsp) oil plus a little for brushing
2.5 ml (½ level tsp) salt
a little ghee (page 113) or butter

STUFFING
200 ml (⅓ pint) finely chopped fresh coriander leaves
10 ml (2 level tsp) coriander-cumin seed powder (dhana-jira, page 113)
1.25 ml (¼ level tsp) turmeric powder
15 ml (1 level tbsp) gram flour (besan)
3 green chillies, ground or finely chopped
salt

Mix all the ingredients for the stuffing and season with salt. Divide into 8 equal portions.

Mix the wholemeal flour, oil and salt and add enough water to make a soft dough. Knead well and divide into 8 equal portions.

Roll out each dough portion very thinly on a lightly floured surface into 15–20 cm (6–8 inch) diameter circles. Brush with a little oil and sprinkle the stuffing portion uniformly.

Make a small hole in the centre with your finger and start rolling the dough outwards in all directions towards the periphery while stretching it at the same time so that the inner diameter constantly increases. Finally when a thin circular roll along the outer diameter is left, break the roll. Now roll this bread stick-like dough from centre outwards into the shape of a Catherine wheel (a continuous circular line of ever-increasing diameter). Press by hand and flatten. Roll out again into a thin roti of 15–20 cm (6–8 inch) diameter. Repeat for the remaining dough and filling.

Cook the rotis in a non-greased heavy-based frying pan or griddle (tawa). When small brown spots appear on the surface turn the rotis and cook on the other side. Spread with ghee or butter and serve hot.

LEFT *Coriander Roti (see above)*
CENTRE *Malaysian-style Parathas (see page 70)*
RIGHT *Spicy Puris (see page 62)*

65

PLAIN PARATHAS
▬ *Sade parathe* ▬

Makes 10–12 parathas
Preparation time: 10 minutes
Cooking time: 30 minutes

These plain parathas for day-to-day use go very well with dals and vegetables.

350 g (12 oz) wholemeal flour (gehun ka atta)
2.5 ml (½ level tsp) salt
30 ml (2 tbsp) ghee (page 113) plus melted ghee for brushing

Sift the flour with the salt. Add the 30 ml (2 tbsp) ghee and enough water to make a soft dough. Knead the dough for 3–4 minutes. Divide into 10–12 portions.

Roll out into 12.5–15 cm (5–6 inches) diameter rounds and brush with melted ghee. Fold each portion into half and again roll out into a triangular shape.

Cook one paratha at a time on a hot tawa (griddle), turning once. After a minute, add a little ghee around the edges of the paratha, which should swell up. Turn again and fry the other side. The paratha is ready when brown patches appear on both sides. Serve hot.

MINTY CORN AND VEGETABLE PARATHAS
▬ *Makai phudina aur tarkari parathe* ▬

Makes about 15 parathas
Preparation time: 20 minutes
Cooking time: 40 minutes

The inclusion of mint gives these parathas a very special, fresh flavour. Serve with natural yogurt (dahi, page 114).

175 g (6 oz) plain flour (maida)
175 g (6 oz) wholemeal flour (gehun ka atta)
15 ml (1 tbsp) melted ghee (page 113) plus ghee for cooking

STUFFING
100 g (4 oz) cabbage, finely chopped
salt
250 g (9 oz) fresh or frozen corn kernels
15 ml (1 tbsp) oil
2 medium potatoes, peeled and roughly chopped
1 medium onion, peeled and finely chopped
juice of 1 lemon
2.5 ml (½ level tsp) garam masala (page 116)
15 ml (1 tbsp) finely chopped fresh coriander leaves
5 ml (1 tsp) ground green chilli
5 ml (1 level tsp) sugar

BREADS

MINT SAUCE
25 g (1 oz) mint leaves
5 ml (1 tsp) lemon juice
2.5 ml (½ level tsp) cumin seeds
3 green chillies
5 ml (1 level tsp) salt
100 ml (4 fl oz) water

Sprinkle salt over the cabbage and leave for 10 minutes. Meanwhile, boil the corn kernels, simmer for about 10 minutes until tender then drain and crush. Squeeze the water from the cabbage with your hands.

Heat the oil in a large pan and add the potatoes. Sprinkle over a little water, cover and cook until soft. Add the cabbage and onion and cook for 1 minute more. Add the corn, lemon juice, garam masala, coriander, green chilli and sugar. Season with salt and mix, then remove from the heat.

Blend the ingredients for the sauce in a blender or food processor.

Mix the flours and ghee with the mint sauce to make a soft dough, adding water if necessary. Divide into about 15 equal portions and roll out very thinly into 15 cm (6 inch) rounds. Cook the rounds very lightly in a heavy-based frying pan or griddle (tawa). When small brown spots appear on the surface turn the parathas and cook the other side.

To serve, put 30 ml (2 tbsp) of the stuffing in the centre of each paratha. Fold the paratha towards the centre from all 4 sides and press to seal. Cook in a heavy-based frying pan or griddle (tawa) lightly brushed with ghee. When small brown spots appear on the surface turn the parathas and cook the other side. Serve hot.

KIDNEY BEAN PARATHAS
Rajma ke parathe

BREADS

The Indian red kidney bean is very similar to the Mexican variety. If you like you can substitute the stuffing mixture with canned refried beans, and the sauces with Mexican green and hot sauces.

Makes about 8–10 parathas
Preparation time: 30 minutes plus 10 hours soaking
Cooking time: 1 hour 30 minutes

450 g (1 lb) wholemeal flour (gehun ka atta) or plain flour (maida)
2.5 ml (½ level tsp) salt
10 ml (2 tsp) butter
oil for cooking
chilli sauce
finely chopped spring onions

STUFFING
150 g (5 oz) red kidney beans (rajma)
30 ml (2 tbsp) ghee (page 113)
15 ml (1 tbsp) butter
2 medium onions, peeled and finely chopped
5 ml (1 level tsp) chilli powder
5 ml (1 level tsp) roasted cumin seed powder (page 118)
45–60 ml (3–4 tbsp) tomato ketchup
salt

GREEN SAUCE
4 green tomatoes
150 ml (¼ pint) water
1 large onion, peeled and roughly chopped
3–4 green chillies, roughly chopped
10 ml (2 tsp) vinegar
salt

Put the kidney beans into a bowl, cover with cold water and leave to soak for 8–10 hours. Drain the beans, cover with fresh cold water and bring to the boil. Boil for 10 minutes then lower the heat and simmer for 1 hour until tender. Drain thoroughly.

Heat the ghee and 15 ml (1 tbsp) butter in a saucepan and fry the onions for 1 minute. Add the beans, chilli powder, cumin powder and tomato ketchup and season with salt.

To make the green sauce: boil the tomatoes with the water. Purée in a blender or food processor with the onion, green chillies, vinegar and salt to taste.

Mix the flour and 2.5 ml (½ level tsp) salt with the remaining butter and enough water to make a soft dough. Roll out on a lightly floured surface into small rounds 10–12.5 cm (4–5 inches) in diameter. Cook the parathas in a heavy-based frying pan or griddle (tawa) lightly brushed with oil. When small brown spots appear on the surface, turn the chapatis and cook on the other side.

To serve, first spread a little green sauce over each paratha, then a little stuffing, a dash of chilli sauce, a little more green sauce and finally sprinkle over spring onions. Roll up the stuffed paratha.

Cook the stuffed paratha in a heavy-based frying pan or griddle (tawa) lightly brushed with oil. Cook on both sides until crisp. Serve hot.

CABBAGE AND SOFT CHEESE PARATHAS

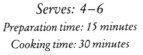

Gobhi aur paneer ke parathe

Stuffed parathas make a substantial meal, so are often eaten for breakfast or brunch. For this particular version, the filling requires no cooking. Serve with natural yogurt (dahi, page 114).

Serves: 4–6
Preparation time: 15 minutes
Cooking time: 30 minutes

250 g (9 oz) wholemeal flour (gehun ka atta) or plain flour (maida)
2.5 ml (½ level tsp) salt
15 ml (1 tbsp) ghee (page 113) plus extra for cooking
about 225 ml (8 fl oz) water

STUFFING
3.75 ml (¾ level tsp) salt plus extra for seasoning
225 g (8 oz) cabbage, grated
100 g (4 oz) soft cheese, crumbled (paneer, page 114)
30 ml (2 tbsp) finely chopped fresh coriander leaves
2 green chillies, finely chopped

Sift the flour with the salt. Add the 15 ml (1 tbsp) ghee to the flour and add enough water to make a soft dough. Knead the dough for 3–4 minutes and divide into 10 portions.

To make the stuffing: sprinkle the salt over the cabbage, mix well and leave for 10 minutes. Squeeze out the water by pressing the cabbage with both hands. Mix the cabbage with the soft cheese (paneer), coriander and chillies. Season with salt.

Roll out the dough into small rounds of 10 cm (4 inch) diameter. Spread a little filling on one round and place another round on top. Press the sides well. Cook the parathas in a heavy-based frying pan or griddle (tawa) lightly brushed with ghee. When small brown spots appear on the surface, turn the parathas and cook on the other side. Serve hot.

69

MALAYSIAN-STYLE PARATHAS
■ *Martaba* ■

*Makes about 10
parathas*
Preparation time: 20 minutes
Cooking time: 40 minutes

These stuffed parathas are popular in Singapore and nearby countries.
Serve them with chilli garlic sauce.

250 g (9 oz) plain flour (maida)
15 ml (1 tbsp) oil plus oil for cooking
2.5 ml (½ level tsp) salt

STUFFING
30 ml (2 tbsp) oil
2 medium onions, peeled and sliced
225 g (8 oz) cabbage, grated
75 g (3 oz) carrots, peeled and grated
75 g (3 oz) bean-sprouts
a few drops of soy sauce
2.5 ml (½ level tsp) sugar
salt

Make the stuffing: heat the oil in a large pan, Chinese wok or kadai.
Add the vegetables and cook for 3–4 minutes. Add soy sauce and
sugar and season with salt. Set aside to cool.

Mix the plain flour with the oil and salt and add enough water to
make a soft dough. Knead well and roll out on a lightly floured surface
into paper thin parathas, about 25–30 cm (10–12 inches) diameter.

Put about 30 ml (2 tbsp) of the vegetable stuffing into the centre of
each paratha. Spread a little and fold in all the sides.

Cook the parathas in a heavy-based frying pan or griddle (tawa)
lightly brushed with oil. When small brown spots appear on the
surface, turn the parathas and cook on the other side. Repeat with the
remaining parathas and stuffing.

DOUBLE-DECKER PARATHAS
Gajar aur mutter paratha

BREADS

These parathas are both tasty and nutritious and with their two stuffings, also look pleasingly colourful.

450 g (1 lb) wholemeal flour (gehun ka atta)
30 ml (2 tbsp) melted ghee, plus ghee for cooking (page 113)
2.5 ml (½ level tsp) salt

Makes 7 parathas
Preparation time: 20 minutes
Cooking time: 30 minutes

CARROT STUFFING
5 ml (1 tbsp) ghee (page 113) or butter
5 ml (1 level tsp) cumin seeds
3 medium carrots, peeled and grated
2 green chillies, finely chopped
5 ml (1 tsp) lemon juice
salt

GREEN PEA STUFFING
225 g (8 oz) shelled green peas
15 ml (1 tbsp) ghee (page 113)
5 ml (1 level tsp) cumin seeds
15 ml (1 tbsp) finely chopped fresh coriander leaves
2 green chillies, finely chopped
10 ml (2 level tsp) amchur powder
salt

Mix the wholemeal flour with the ghee and salt and add sufficient water to make a soft dough. Knead very well.

To make the carrot stuffing: heat the ghee in a pan and fry the cumin seeds for 30 seconds or until they turn brown. Add the carrots, chillies and lemon juice. Season with salt and mix well. Cover and cook for 2 minutes, then set aside to cool.

To make the green pea stuffing: boil the peas then drain and mash. Heat the ghee in a pan and fry the cumin seeds for 30 seconds. Add the remaining ingredients, season with salt and cook for 1 minute. Cool.

Divide the dough into 21 portions and roll out into rounds of equal size. Cook 7 rounds in a heavy-based frying pan or griddle (tawa). When brown spots appear, turn and cook on the other side.

On one uncooked round, spread 15 ml (1 tbsp) of the carrot filling. Cover with a cooked round and spread over 15 ml (1 tbsp) of the green pea stuffing. Put another uncooked round on top and press down to seal the edges well. Cook the double-decker paratha in a heavy-based frying pan or griddle (tawa) lightly brushed with ghee. When brown spots appear underneath, turn and cook on the other side. Repeat with the remaining rounds and stuffing. Serve hot.

71

SPICY PARATHAS
▰ *Masaledar parathe* ▰

Makes: 12–14 parathas
Preparation time: 20 minutes
plus 2 hours soaking
Cooking time: 30 minutes

A simple but delightfully spicy variety of parathas.

350 g (12 oz) wholemeal flour (gehun ka atta)
30 ml (2 tbsp) ghee (page 113) plus ghee for cooking
2.5 ml (½ level tsp) salt

STUFFING
60 ml (4 level tbsp) poppy seeds (khus-khus)
10 ml (2 level tsp) cumin seeds
1.25 ml (¼ level tsp) asafoetida powder
4 red chillies
seeds of 4 cardamoms
4 cloves
2×1 cm (½ inch) cinnamon sticks
10 ml (2 tsp) ghee (page 113)
2.5 ml (½ level tsp) nigella seeds (kalonji)
2.5 ml (½ level tsp) ground ginger
salt

Soak the poppy seeds for the stuffing in a small quantity of water for 2 hours.

For the parathas: mix the flour, ghee and salt and add enough water to make a soft dough. Knead thoroughly and set aside for 30 minutes.

Meanwhile, put the cumin seeds, asafoetida, chillies, cardamoms, cloves and cinnamon sticks into a heavy-based pan or griddle (tawa) and dry roast for 2 minutes, then grind to a fine powder in a coffee grinder.

Put the poppy seeds into a blender or food processor and blend to a paste with a little water.

Heat the ghee in a small pan and fry the nigella seeds and ginger for 30 seconds. Add the poppy seed paste and continue cooking for 1 minute. Remove from the heat and add the powdered spices.

Divide the dough into 12–14 balls. On a lightly floured board, roll out into 7.5 cm (3 inch) diameter rounds, spread 5 ml (1 tsp) of the stuffing evenly over each and fold the circles in half. Again spread over a little stuffing and fold into a quarter circle. Seal the edges with a little paste made of flour and water. On a lightly floured surface, roll out into triangular parathas.

Cook in a hot heavy-based frying pan or griddle (tawa) lightly brushed with ghee. When small brown spots appear on the surface, turn the parathas and cook on the other side. Serve hot.

LAYERED CHAPATI BAKE
◢ Bake chapati ◣

Try this novel way of stuffing and baking chapatis as an alternative to
the traditional one.

175 g (6 oz) wholemeal flour (gehun ka atta)
15 ml (1 tbsp) ghee (page 113) or butter
2.5 ml (½ level tsp) salt
milk for the dough, plus 100 ml (4 fl oz)
10 ml (2 level tsp) plain flour (maida)
10 ml (2 tsp) melted butter

STUFFING
2 medium potatoes, peeled
175 g (6 oz) mixed vegetables (eg French beans, carrots, cauliflower),
  finely chopped
30 ml (2 tbsp) butter or ghee (page 113)
1 medium onion, peeled and finely chopped
1 medium tomato, finely chopped
1 green chilli, finely chopped
5 ml (1 level tsp) chilli powder
1.25 ml (¼ level tsp) turmeric powder
15 ml (1 tbsp) chopped cashew nuts
15 ml (1 tbsp) finely chopped fresh coriander leaves
salt

BREADS

Serves: 6–8
Preparation time: 15 minutes
Cooking time: 30 minutes

Boil the potatoes, drain, mash and set aside. Put all the chopped
vegetables into one pan with just enough water to cover and bring to
the boil. Simmer until tender, then drain and set aside. To make the
chapatis: mix the wholemeal flour and ghee or butter. Add the salt and
enough milk to make a soft dough, then knead for 5 minutes.

Roll out the dough on a lightly floured surface into thin chapatis
about 15 cm (6 inches) in diameter. Cook the chapatis in a heavy-based
frying pan or griddle (tawa) lightly brushed with ghee. When small
brown spots appear, turn the chapatis and cook on the other side.

To make the stuffing: heat the butter or ghee in a large pan and fry
the onion for 1 minute. Add the tomato and green chilli and fry for
1 minute more, then add the potatoes, mixed vegetables and remaining
ingredients for the stuffing. Season with salt and keep warm.

Heat the oven to fairly hot, 200°C/400°F/Gas mark 6. Mix the
100 ml (4 fl oz) milk and the plain flour. Lay a chapati in an ungreased
baking dish and spread a little stuffing on top. Dip another chapati in
the flour and milk mixture and place on top of the stuffing. Spread a
little more stuffing on top. Continue ending with a dipped chapati.
Pour over the butter and bake for 15 minutes. Cut into wedges.

SALADS AND
ACCOMPANIMENTS

Although traditional Indian cooking does not have Western-style salads, a variety of contrasting tastes and textures is introduced into a meal by the accompaniments served. These include kachumbers, raitas, achars, chutneys, papads and khichiya. Since there are literally hundreds of different combinations of all these dishes, the imaginative cook can easily enliven even simple meals.

Kachumbers are combinations of chopped raw or cooked vegetables with seasoning. Raitas, or yogurt relishes, are mixtures of natural yogurt and vegetables, such as cucumber slices and seasoning. Achars or pickles include such vegetables as onions in a spicy sauce; chutneys, in which fresh vegetables are ground with spices and papads and khichiya.

FRUIT AND BEAN SALAD
◾ *Shahi salad* ◾

In this satisfying, protein-rich salad, the combinations of fruit and pulses can be varied to suit personal tastes.

100 g (4 oz) green chick peas (hare chane)
100 g (4 oz) moong dal
100 g (4 oz) math
50 g (2 oz) white chick peas (kabuli chane)
4 chikoos, peeled, seeded and diced
100 g (4 oz) skinned peanuts
2 eating apples, peeled, cored and diced
4 oranges, peeled, segmented and diced
175 g (6 oz) green grapes, seeded and quartered
2 radishes, diced
2 carrots, peeled and diced
a few salad leaves, roughly chopped
a few spinach leaves, roughly chopped
2 green chillies, finely chopped
5 ml (1 level tsp) ginger powder
salt

DRESSING
400 ml (⅔ pint) natural yogurt (dahi, page 114)
30 ml (2 tbsp) chopped mint leaves
5 ml (1 level tsp) sugar
5 ml (1 level tsp) salt (optional)

Serves: 8
Preparation time: 20 minutes
plus 6 hours soaking
and 24 hours sprouting
Cooking time: 30 minutes

Put all the pulses and the peanuts into a large bowl, cover with cold water and leave to soak for at least 6 hours. Drain thoroughly and tie them in a piece of muslin, then set aside for 24 hours until they start to sprout. Discard the muslin, put the sprouted peanuts and pulses into a pan and cover with water. Bring to the boil then cover, simmer for about 30 minutes or until soft.

Combine the peanuts and pulses with the fruits, vegetables, salad leaves, spinach leaves, green chillies and ginger powder. Season with salt to taste. Mix thoroughly and leave to chill.

Prepare the dressing. Mix the yogurt, mint leaves, sugar and salt, if wished, and leave to chill. Just before serving, toss the salad and serve the dressing in a separate bowl.

BEETROOT, CUCUMBER AND
TOMATO RAITA
Chukandar kheera aur tamatar ka raita

This cooling raita is both colourful and crunchy.

Serves: 6
Preparation time: 15 minutes
Cooking time: 1 minute

400 ml (⅔ pint) natural yogurt (dahi, page 114)
1 beetroot, boiled, peeled and cubed
2 medium cucumbers, cubed
2 medium tomatoes, cubed
45 ml (3 tbsp) roughly chopped peanuts
30 ml (2 tbsp) finely chopped fresh coriander leaves
5 ml (1 tsp) chopped green chilli
30 ml (2 tbsp) grated fresh or flaked coconut
5 ml (1 level tsp) caster sugar
salt
10 ml (2 tsp) oil
5 ml (1 level tsp) cumin seeds
2 pinches of asafoetida powder

Beat the yogurt and add the vegetables, peanuts, coriander leaves, green chilli, coconut and sugar. Season with salt.

Heat the oil in a small pan and fry the cumin seeds until they splutter. Add the asafoetida then pour over the raita.

BANANA AND
CUCUMBER KACHUMBAR
Kele aur kheera ki kachumbar

This sweet and sour, crunchy cucumber dish goes well with rice and curry.

Serves: 6
Preparation time: 10 minutes
plus 30 minutes chilling
No cooking

3 ripe bananas
3 medium or 1 large cucumber, diced
10 ml (2 tsp) lemon juice
2 green chillies, finely chopped
45 ml (3 tbsp) roughly ground peanuts
30 ml (2 tbsp) finely chopped fresh coriander leaves
30 ml (2 tbsp) grated fresh or flaked coconut
3.75 ml (1½ level tsp) caster sugar
salt

Peel and dice the bananas and mix with the cucumbers. Immediately add the lemon juice and mix well. Add the remaining ingredients and chill for 30 minutes. Serve cold.

GREEN CHICK PEA SALAD
Hare chane ka salad

If you have difficulty buying the green chick peas needed for this
colourful and tasty salad, you can substitute fresh or canned chick peas.
Serve with corn chips, if wished.

175 g (6 oz) green chick peas (hare chane)
1 medium potato, peeled
1 medium tomato, roughly chopped
30 ml (2 tbsp) finely chopped fresh coriander leaves
2 green chillies, finely chopped
1.25–2.5 ml (¼–½ level tsp) black salt (sanchal)
15 ml (1 tbsp) lemon juice
10 ml (2 level tsp) sugar
10 ml (2 level tsp) chaat masala (page 119)
salt

Serves: 4–6
Preparation time: 10 minutes
plus 6–7 hours soaking
Cooking time: 1 hour
15 minutes

Put the green chick peas into a bowl, cover with cold water and leave
to soak for at least 6–7 hours. Drain the green chick peas and cover
with fresh cold water. Bring to the boil, then simmer for 1 hour until
tender.

   Boil the potato, drain and cool, then cut into cubes.

   When the green chick peas are cooked, drain thoroughly and mix in
the cubed potato with the remaining ingredients. Salt to taste, set aside
to cool, then leave to chill.

   Just before serving, sprinkle with a few corn chips, if wished.

BLACK-EYED BEAN SALAD
◀ *Lobhia* ▶

A tasty alternative to this recipe can be made by substituting the black-eyed beans with cooked white chick peas and the dressing by chaat masala (page 119).

Serves: 6
Preparation time: 10 minutes
plus 4 hours soaking
Cooking time: 15 minutes

175 g (6 oz) black-eyed beans (lobhia)
1 medium tomato, finely chopped
1 medium onion, peeled and finely chopped
1 green pepper, seeded and finely chopped
1 medium cucumber, finely chopped
1 green chilli, finely chopped
15 ml (1 tbsp) finely chopped fresh coriander leaves
15 ml (1 tbsp) oil
5 ml (1 tsp) lemon juice
2.5 ml (½ level tsp) sugar
15 ml (1 level tsp) salt

Put the beans into a bowl, cover with cold water and leave to soak for 4 hours. Drain and boil them until cooked. Drain. Add the tomato, onion, green pepper, cucumber, green chilli and coriander leaves.

Mix the oil, lemon juice and sugar. Season with salt and pour over the salad. Chill and serve.

COCONUT CHUTNEY
Nariyal chutney

This chutney goes well with dosas, idlis, wadas and other South Indian dishes.

60 ml (4 tbsp) flaked or grated fresh coconut
60 ml (4 level tbsp) roasted and puffed split yellow chick peas
  (bhuje hooey chane ki dal)
3 small green chillies
30 ml (2 tbsp) finely chopped fresh coriander leaves
4–5 curry leaves
30 ml (2 tbsp) water
10 ml (2 tsp) oil
2.5 ml (½ level tsp) mustard seeds
1 small red chilli
pinch of asafoetida powder (optional)
45 ml (3 tbsp) natural yogurt (dahi, page 114)
salt

Put the coconut, split chick peas, green chillies, coriander leaves, 2 curry leaves and the water into a blender or food processor and blend for a few seconds, taking care not to grind finely.

Heat the oil in a small pan and fry the mustard seeds until they splutter. Add 2–3 curry leaves, the red chilli and asafoetida. After a few seconds, pour over the coconut mixture, add the yogurt and season with salt.

SALADS AND
ACCOMPANI-
MENTS

Serves: 8–10
Preparation time: 5 minutes
Cooking time: 2 minutes

NATURAL YOGURT SAUCE
◼ *Masala dahi* ◼

*Makes 600 ml (1 pint)
sauce*
*Preparation time: 5 minutes
plus 30 minutes soaking*
Cooking time: a few minutes

This sauce goes very well with chapatis and rice.

5 ml (1 level tsp) long-grain rice
5 ml (1 level tsp) toovar dal
200 ml (⅓ pint) water
2 small green chillies
5 mm (¼ inch) piece fresh ginger, peeled
*2.5 cm (1 inch) square fresh coconut or 15 ml (1 tbsp) flaked or grated
   fresh coconut*
600 ml (1 pint) thick fresh natural yogurt (dahi, page 114)
2 pinches of turmeric powder
salt
10 ml (2 tsp) oil
2.5 ml (½ level tsp) mustard seeds
1 small red chilli
3–4 curry leaves
1 small onion, peeled and finely chopped

Soak the rice and dal in the water for 30 minutes. To the soaked
mixture, add the chillies, ginger and coconut. Put into a blender or
food processor and blend.

Beat the yogurt and add the rice and dal mixture and turmeric
powder. Season with salt.

Heat the oil in a small pan and fry the mustard seeds until they
splutter. Add the red chilli, curry leaves, onion and seasoned yogurt
and cook for 30 seconds. Cool and serve.

Fruit and Bean Salad (see page 75)

FRUIT CHAAT
◀ *Phal ka chaat* ▶

Vary the fruit and vegetable combination in this chaat according to
your own preferences.

8–10 grapes, halved and seeded
1 banana, skinned and chopped
1 apple, peeled and cubed
1 guava, peeled and cubed
1 ripe mango, peeled and cubed
1 medium tomato, chopped
1 medium boiled potato, cubed
1 medium cucumber, peeled and chopped
1 green pepper, seeded and chopped
5 ml (1 tsp) lemon juice
15 ml (1 tbsp) chaat masala (page 119)
15 ml (1 tbsp) finely chopped fresh coriander leaves
salt

Serves: 6
Preparation time: 10 minutes
plus 30 minutes chilling
No cooking

Mix all the fruit and vegetables together and pour the lemon juice on
top. Sprinkle over the chaat masala and coriander leaves. Season with
salt and chill in the refrigerator for 30 minutes. Serve cold.

FRUIT CHUTNEY
◀ *Phal ki chutney* ▶

A sweet and sour chutney, using whichever fruit you prefer.

45 ml (3 tbsp) tamarind paste
45 ml (3 level tbsp) sugar
200 ml (⅓ pint) water
200 ml (⅓ pint) mixed chopped fruit
5 ml (1 level tsp) chilli powder
5 ml (1 level tsp) roasted cumin seed powder (page 118)
2.5 ml (½ level tsp) black salt (sanchal)
salt

Makes about 300 ml
(½ pint)
Preparation time: 10 minutes
Cooking time: 10 minutes

Mix the tamarind paste, sugar and water and put on to boil. Boil for
3 minutes, then remove from the heat. Add the fruit, chilli powder,
cumin seed powder and black salt. Season with salt.

TOP *Black-eyed Bean Salad (see page 78)*
LEFT *Beetroot, Cucumber and Tomato Raital (see page 76)*
RIGHT *Natural Yogurt Sauce (see page 80)*

SWEET DISHES

In India it is not usual to serve sweet dishes at meal times – they are usually offered to visiting guests, at breakfast time, or with tea. In the winter months, special sweets and paks considered good for the health are served, while sweets such as pedas and laddoos are given to celebrate good news.

Simple sweet dishes are made at home, but as many other Indian sweets are time-consuming or complicated to make, it is not uncommon to buy ready-made sweetmeats from the halwais (sweetmeat specialists).

A number of sweet dishes are made from milk. In some, milk is concentrated until semi-solid (that is using khoya) whereas in others, the constituents are separated, for example by adding alum or citric acid. Nuts, saffron and rose water are commonly used and items like vark (thin silver leaf) and rose petals are often used for decoration.

ALMOND SWEET
◀ *Badam ki chakki* ▶

This rich sweet is traditionally served on special occasions like weddings.

900 g (2 lb) whole, unblanched almonds
900 g (2 lb) sugar
silver leaf (vark)

Makes 15 pieces
Preparation time: 15 minutes
plus 12 hours soaking
Cooking time: 15 minutes

Soak the almonds in water for 12 hours, then drain and put them into boiling water. Cover and leave for 10 minutes.

Drain the almonds, remove the skins and drop into cold water so that the almonds do not discolour.

Grind the almonds with a little water in a coffee grinder. Add the sugar and cook in a large pan on a medium heat until the mixture forms into a dough. Leave for 5 minutes.

Roll out the dough, mark into shapes and decorate with silver leaf.

ALMOND-PISTACHIO ROLL
◀ *Badam pista roll* ▶

This royal sweet combines the flavours of almonds and pistachios.

450 g (1 lb) pistachios
225 g (8 oz) sugar
120 ml (8 tbsp) water plus 1.25 ml (¼ tsp) warm water
a pinch of saffron (optional)
seeds of 2 green cardamoms, powdered
900 g (2 lb) almond dough (see above)

Makes 10–12 pieces
Preparation time: 20 minutes
Cooking time: 30 minutes

Put the pistachios into boiling water for 3–4 minutes. Drain and remove the skins by rubbing on a cloth. Grind into a powder.

Mix the sugar and the 120 ml (8 tbsp) water and bring to the boil in a large pan until it forms a soft ball mixture. Add the pistachio powder and leave to cool.

Put the saffron into a cup with the warm water and rub until it dissolves. Add to the pistachio dough with the cardamom powder. Make small rolls from this dough.

Roll out the almond dough and cut into pieces which exactly cover the pistachio rolls.

Put a pistachio roll inside a cut almond dough piece and roll up. Repeat with the remaining pistachio rolls and almond dough pieces. Cut into small pieces and serve.

ALMOND FIG SWEET

Badam anjir sweet

Makes about 20 pieces
Preparation time: 20 minutes
plus 4 hours soaking
Cooking time: 15 minutes

This is a light tea-time sweet. You can replace the green figs with other fleshy, mild-flavoured fruits, like the Indian chikoos.

100 g (4 oz) almonds
30 ml (2 tbsp) milk
125 g (4 oz) sugar
1 drop rose essence (kewara)
a little ghee (page 113)
2 fresh figs about 50 g (2 oz), finely chopped
50 g (2 oz) milk concentrate (khoya, page 118)
silver leaf (vark)

Soak the almonds in water for 4 hours, then drain and remove the skins. Put the almonds and the milk into a blender or food processor and blend into a smooth paste. Mix in 75 g (3 oz) sugar.

Pour the almond paste into a small deep pan (kadai) and heat gently, stirring, until the liquid is absorbed and the mixture does not stick to the back of the finger. Be careful to keep the heat low or the mixture will discolour. Add the essence.

Knead the almond paste using a little ghee for greasing if needed. Roll out the paste with a rolling pin into an oval shape on a wooden board greased with ghee. Trim into a rectangular shape.

Put the figs in a muslin cloth or strainer and dip into boiling water for about 30 seconds to soften. Add the remaining sugar with the milk concentrate (khoya) to the figs. Cook as for the almond paste.

Roll out the fig paste with a rolling pin into an oval shape on a wooden board greased with ghee. Trim to the same rectangular shape as the almond paste and place on top of the almond paste. Lift the end and fold the paste into two. Using the almond trimmed portions, seal so that the fig portion is completely concealed. Roll out with the hands applying a little pressure until the roll is long and thin.

Cut the roll into equal pieces of about 5 cm (2 inches). Using a sharp knife cut the silver leaf to the same length as the pieces. Roll up the individual almond rolls in the silver leaf.

INDIAN-STYLE SAFFRON CHEESE PIE
◀ Kesari paneer cake ▶

SWEET DISHES

This hot cheese pie, with its delicious combination of paneer and saffron, is a successful combination of Indian and Western cookery.

2 pinches of saffron
1.25 ml (¼ tsp) warm water plus 15 ml (1 tbsp) water
225 g (8 oz) soft cheese (paneer, page 114)
150 ml (¼ pint) milk
75 g (3 oz) caster sugar plus 10 ml (2 level tsp) caster sugar
2.5 ml (½ level tsp) baking powder
seeds of 2 cardamoms, powdered
75 g (3 oz) apples, peeled, cored and sliced
blanched and sliced almonds and pistachios, to decorate

Serves: 6
Preparation time: 15 minutes
Cooking time: 30 minutes

Heat the oven to 180°C/350°F/Gas mark 4. Put the saffron into a cup with 1.25 ml (¼ tsp) warm water and rub until it dissolves.

Put the soft cheese, milk, saffron, 75 g (3 oz) sugar and the 15 ml (1 tbsp) water into a blender or food processor and blend until light and fluffy. Taste the mixture and, if required, add additional sugar. Add the baking powder and cardamom powder.

Arrange the sliced apples in a baking tin 15–17.5 cm (6–7 inches) deep. Sprinkle the 10 ml (2 level tsp) sugar over the apples and spread the soft cheese mixture on top. Bake in the oven for 25–30 minutes.

Decorate with sliced almonds and pistachios. Cut into pieces and serve warm, spooning over the saffron syrup.

SWEET CHEESE WITH FRUIT
Shahi kesar tukde phal ke saath

Serves: 8
Preparation time: 10 minutes
plus
1 hours chilling
Cooking time: 30 minutes

Serve this chilled cheese with a mixture of fresh fruits.

2 litres (3½ pints) milk plus 30 ml (2 tbsp) milk
150 g (5 oz) sugar
3 pinches of citric acid
10 ml (2 level tsp) cornflour
2 pinches of saffron
1.25 ml (¼ tsp) warm water
1.25 ml (¼ level tsp) cardamom powder
fresh fruit, to serve

Heat the 2 litres (3½ pints) milk with the sugar in a large heavy-based, non-stick pan or Chinese wok on a high heat for 10–15 minutes. When the milk starts boiling, add the citric acid. Cook until the mixture is reduced to half in quantity.

Mix the cornflour with the 30 ml (2 tbsp) milk. Add to the mixture and cook for at least 5–6 minutes.

Put the saffron into a cup with the water and rub until it dissolves. Add to the mixture.

Remove from the heat and cool. Then add the cardamom powder. Pour into ice cube trays and chill in the refrigerator for at least an hour. Serve with fresh fruit salad.

DOUBLE-DECKER SWEET
Badam pista mithai

Serves: 8–10
Preparation time: 15 minutes
Cooking time: 30–40 minutes

The secret of this rich and colourful barfi lies in cooking it very fast on a high heat.

30 ml (2 tbsp) almonds
30 ml (2 tbsp) pistachios
2 litres (3½ pints) full-fat milk
225 g (8 oz) sugar
1 small piece of alum or 2 pinches of powdered alum
2 pinches of saffron
1.25 ml (¼ tsp) warm water
a little green food colouring

Put the almonds into hot water for 10 minutes, then drain, remove the skins and chop very finely. Chop the pistachios (with their skins) very finely.

Pour the milk into a large non-stick pan and heat on high. When it starts boiling, add the sugar and stir well for 3 minutes.

Add the alum and continue boiling until the milk becomes very thick. Test 2.5 ml (½ tsp) of the mixture on a plate – if it forms a soft ball, remove from the heat. When the mixture solidifies, divide into two.

Put the saffron into a cup with the water and rub until it dissolves. Add the saffron liquid and almonds to one part of the milk mixture and the pistachios and a few drops of green colour to the other. Mix each part well.

Grease a small plate and spread one part evenly over the surface. Spread the other part on top. Cool, then cut into pieces and serve.

MANGO VANILLA BARFI
◣ *Aam barfi* ◢

This light barfi is made from milk in contrast to the standard barfis made from khoya. If you prefer, you can omit the paneer layer.

1 litre (1¾ pints) milk
150 g (5 oz) sugar
a pinch of alum powder
60 ml (4 tbsp) mango juice (alphonso)
175 g (6 oz) soft cheese (paneer, page 114)
45 ml (3 level tbsp) caster sugar
2.5 ml (½ tsp) vanilla essence
chopped almonds and pistachios, to decorate

Makes 10–12 pieces
Preparation time: 10 minutes
Cooking time: 20 minutes

To make the mango barfi: put the milk into a large pan and bring to the boil on a high heat. When it starts to boil, add the sugar. After 2 minutes, add the alum and continue boiling until the mixture becomes thick.

Test about 2.5 ml (½ tsp) of the mixture on a plate – if it forms a soft ball, add the mango juice. Continue cooking for at least 4–5 minutes. Test again and when the mixture forms a ball, remove from the heat.

Spread the mixture on a flat plate (thali) and allow to cool.

Sieve the soft cheese and add the sugar and essence. Cook in a pan on a low heat for 2–3 minutes.

Spread a layer of soft cheese over the mango mixture. Sprinkle the chopped nuts on top and chill in the refrigerator. To serve, cut into decorative pieces.

PISTACHIO BARFI
Pista barfi

A rich delicately coloured sweet that is ideal for special occasions.

Makes 15 pieces
Preparation time: 15 minutes
Cooking time: 15 minutes

500 g (1 lb) pistachios
1 kg (2 lb) sugar
300 ml (10 fl oz) water
250 g (10 oz) milk concentrate (khoya, page 118)
a few drops of rose water (kewara) or pistachio essence (optional)
2.5 ml (½ level tsp) cardamom powder
silver leaf (vark)

Put the pistachios into boiling water for 3–4 minutes. Drain and remove the skin by rubbing on a cloth. Grind the pistachios into powder in a small coffee grinder.

Mix the sugar with 300 ml (10 fl oz) water and boil in a large pan on a medium heat until it reaches the hard ball stage 130°C (265°F).

Sieve the milk concentrate (khoya) and add to the sugar. Cook for 3–4 minutes and then add the pistachio powder and mix well. Add the essence and the cardamom powder. Leave for 12 minutes, then spread on a plate. Mark into the desired shapes and decorate with silver leaf.

APPLE KHEER
Sev ki kheer

Kheer is an extremely popular and traditional Indian sweet made of milk with rice or vermicelli. This is a very quick and tasty version using apple instead of rice. Take care to use sweet dessert apples for this dish and to adjust the sugar to your taste.

Serves: 4–6
Preparation time: 5 minutes
Cooking time: 20 minutes

1 litre (1¾ pints) milk
60 ml (4 tbsp) sugar
3 medium dessert apples, cored and peeled
2.5 ml (½ level tsp) cardamom powder
3 almonds, blanched and sliced

Put the milk on to boil in a heavy-based wide pan. Add the sugar and cook gently until the mixture is reduced by half.

Grate the apples and add to the milk. Bring to the boil and remove from the heat at once. Sprinkle cardamom and almonds on top and serve hot.

GRAM FLOUR SEERA
Besan seera

Seeras are sweet dishes served on very special occasions. One of the richest is made from moong dal, but it is laborious to prepare. This one, which tastes just as good, can be made simply and quickly.

30 ml (2 tbsp) milk plus 150 ml (¼ pint) milk, plus 1.25 (¼ tsp) warm milk
75 ml (5 tbsp) melted ghee (page 113)
125 g (4 oz) gram flour (besan)
150 ml (¼ pint) water
75 g (3 oz) caster sugar
2 pinches of saffron
seeds of 4–5 cardamoms, crushed
5–6 blanched almonds, chopped

SWEET DISHES

Serves: 6
Preparation time: 15 minutes
Cooking time: 20 minutes

Mix the 30 ml (2 tbsp) milk with 15 ml (1 tbsp) ghee and rub the mixture thoroughly into the flour. Set aside for 10 minutes then sieve using a coarse sieve.

Heat 60 ml (4 tbsp) ghee in a large frying pan and add the flour. Cook, stirring, until slightly golden in colour.

In another pan, mix the 150 ml (¼ pint) milk with the water. Heat gently and add to the flour.

Add the sugar and continue cooking and stirring until the ghee separates.

Put the saffron into a cup with the warm milk and rub until it dissolves, then add to the seera. Sprinkle over the cardamoms and chopped almonds and serve hot.

SAFFRON KULFI
Kesar kulfi

Kulfis, the traditional Indian ice creams, are richer than Western ice creams; this is one of the versions of the popular saffron kulfi. It is usually made in special cone-shape aluminium moulds with screw-top lids, but it can be made in ice cube trays instead.

Serves: 6–8
Preparation time: 15 minutes
plus 6–7 hours setting
Cooking time: 30 minutes

2 litres (3½ pints) milk plus 2.5 ml (½ tsp) warm milk
5 ml (1 level tsp) cornflour
90–120 ml (6–8 level tbsp) sugar
10 almonds
15 pistachios
1.25 ml (¼ tsp) saffron
seeds of 8 green cardamoms, crushed
shredded pistachios, to decorate

Beat the 2 litres (3½ pints) milk, cornflour and sugar thoroughly so that no lumps or cornflour remain. Put into a large heavy-based pan and boil until the milk is reduced to less than one-third in volume and the mixture is thick and creamy. Set aside to cool.

Put the nuts into hot water for 10 minutes then drain, remove the skins and chop finely.

Put the saffron into a cup with the warm milk and rub until it dissolves. Add the saffron, chopped nuts and cardamoms to the milk and mix thoroughly. Pour the mixture into kulfi moulds and screw the lids on tightly. Or, pour into a shallow freezer container and cover with foil. Freeze for 6–7 hours or until set.

Just before serving, unmould if in kulfi moulds. Serve in scoops or cut into slices, decorated with shredded pistachios.

SWEET POTATO RABADI
Shakarkand rabadi

A different but nevertheless tasty dish, using sweet potato.

Serves: 4–6
Preparation time: 5 minutes
plus 1 hour chilling
Cooking time: 15 minutes

1 litre (1¾ pints) milk
175 g (6 oz) sweet potatoes, peeled and grated
150 g (5 oz) sugar
a few strands of saffron
1.25 ml (¼ tsp) warm water
2 cardamoms, powdered
2 almonds, blanched and sliced
2 pistachios, blanched and sliced

90

Put the milk into a large pan and bring to the boil. Add the sweet potatoes and continue cooking until the potatoes are tender. Add the sugar and continue cooking for 2 minutes. Remove from the heat and allow to cool.

Put the saffron into a cup with the warm water and rub until it dissolves. Add to the milk mixture. Add the cardamom powder and chill thoroughly for at least 1 hour. Just before serving, sprinkle the almond and pistachio slices on top.

AGAR AGAR SWEET
◄ *Kesari barfi* ►

This popular, light sweet from Gujarat is quickly prepared.

45 ml (3 tbsp) China grass (agar agar), cut into small pieces
150 ml (¼ pint) water plus 1.25 ml (¼ tsp) warm water
600 ml (1 pint) milk
60 ml (4 tbsp) sugar
2 pinches of saffron
2.5 ml (½ level tsp) powdered cardamom
2 almonds, blanched and sliced
2 pistachios, blanched and sliced
rose petals, to decorate (optional)

Serves: 6
Preparation time: 5 minutes
plus 40 minutes setting
Cooking time: 15 minutes

Boil the China grass with the 150 ml (¼ pint) water until the China grass melts.

Put the milk into a large pan and bring to the boil with the sugar. When it starts to boil, add the China grass mixture and boil again for 2 minutes. Strain the mixture.

Put the saffron into a cup with the warm water and rub until it dissolves. Add with the cardamom powder to the China grass mixture and pour into a soup dish or thali. Leave to set for about 30–40 minutes in the refrigerator.

When set, decorate with sliced almonds and pistachios. If you like, sprinkle some rose petals on top. Serve chilled.

SNACKS

As in other Eastern countries, street vendors flourish in India. The vendors sell a wide variety of items ranging from chick peas and peanuts to pakodas, chaats, bhels and paaon bhaji. Many snacks consist of ingredients that are deep-fried in oil or ghee, although some are steamed.

For most Indians, any time is snack-time, and the majority of households have a store of things to eat – both sweet and savoury – usually kept in airtight boxes.

Some snacks are suited for serving with drinks, others for serving at tea time and others, like pakodas, ghugharas and wadas, can also be served as savouries along with the main meal.

MOONG DAL PATTIES
■ *Moong dal tikia* ■

This delicious savoury can be served not only as a snack but also for
lunch or dinner. Serve with green chutney (page 106) or Sonth
(page 106).

175 g (6 oz) moong dal
3 green chillies
45 ml (3 tbsp) natural yogurt (dahi, page 114)
1.25 ml (¼ level tsp) baking powder
a pinch of asafoetida powder
salt
oil for cooking

GREEN PEA STUFFING
100 g (4 oz) shelled green peas
15 ml (1 tbsp) ghee (page 113)
5 ml (1 level tsp) cumin seeds
3 green chillies, finely chopped
15 ml (1 level tbsp) amchur powder
30 ml (2 tbsp) finely chopped fresh coriander leaves
salt

Makes about 20–25
patties
Preparation time: 25 minutes
plus 3–4 hours soaking
Cooking time: 30 minutes

Put the dal into a large bowl, cover with cold water and leave to soak
overnight or for at least 3–4 hours.

Drain the dal and blend in a blender or food processor to a smooth
paste with the green chillies and a little water. Add the yogurt, baking
powder, asafoetida and season with salt.

To make the green pea stuffing: boil the peas, simmer until tender,
then drain and mash. Heat the ghee in a frying pan and fry the cumin
seeds until they splutter. Add the green peas, green chillies and amchur
powder and cook for 1 minute, then add the coriander leaves and
season with salt.

Heat a heavy-based frying pan or griddle (tawa) and drop large
spoonfuls of the dal mixture on to it. Spread it out into 5 cm (2 inch)
rounds and top with a little of the stuffing. Pour a little oil around it
and cook until the underside is brown. Turn and cook the other side.
Repeat with the remaining batter and stuffing and serve hot.

MOONG DAL AND FENUGREEK WAFFLES
Moong dal aur methi bhaji waffle

If fresh fenugreek leaves are not available, use half the quantity of dried fenugreek. Serve with butter and green chutney.

Serves: 4
Preparation time: 10 minutes
plus 4 hours soaking
Cooking time: 20 minutes

175 g (6 oz) moong dal
4 green chillies
25 g (1 oz) finely chopped fenugreek leaves (methi bhaji)
2 pinches of asafoetida powder
1.25 ml (¼ level tsp) bicarbonate of soda or baking powder
15 ml (1 tbsp) oil
5 ml (1 level tsp) sugar
salt

Put the moong dal into a large bowl, cover with cold water and leave to soak for 4 hours. Drain the dal and blend in a blender or food processor to a smooth paste with the green chillies and a little water.

Add the remaining ingredients to make a batter. Pour a little batter in a preheated waffle iron and make waffles. Repeat with the remaining batter. Serve hot.

PAPAD ROLLS
Papad roll

To enjoy their full flavour, eat these rolls hot.

Makes about 20–25
pieces
Preparation time: 30 minutes
Cooking time: 20 minutes

4 medium potatoes, peeled
2 green chillies, finely chopped
2.5 ml (½ level tsp) chilli powder
juice of 1 lemon
30 ml (2 tbsp) finely chopped fresh coriander leaves
2.5 ml (½ level tsp) garam masala (page 116)
2.5 ml (½ level tsp) sugar
salt
8–10 papads
30 ml (2 level tbsp) gram flour (besan)
30 ml (2 tbsp) water
oil for deep frying

Boil the potatoes, drain and mash with the green chillies, chilli powder, lemon juice, coriander leaves, garam masala and sugar. Season with salt

and shape into long rolls about the same length as the diameter of the papad. Dip the papads in water for a few seconds.

Mix the gram flour to a paste with the water. Put a potato roll on the corner of each papad and roll up, then seal with gram flour paste.

Heat the oil in a deep-fat fryer (kadai) and when hot, add the papads in small batches. Cook until golden brown, remove with a slotted spoon, then drain on absorbent kitchen paper. Continue in this way until all the papads have been cooked. Cut into pieces and serve.

CORN AND LENTIL PANCAKES
Spicy paanki

This is an unusual way of cooking and serving food in leaves. If you find it difficult to remove the cooked pancakes from the leaves, add a little gram flour to the remaining mixture.

Makes about 10
pancakes
Preparation time: 25 minutes
plus 4 hours soaking
Cooking time: 15 minutes

100 g (4 oz) moong dal with skins
40 g (1½ oz) urad dal
6 green chillies
100 g (4 oz) cooked tender corn
15 ml (1 level tbsp) gram flour (besan)
2.5 ml (½ level tsp) bicarbonate of soda
2 pinches of asafoetida powder
10 ml (2 tsp) lemon juice
5 ml (1 level tsp) sugar
30 ml (2 tbsp) finely chopped fresh coriander leaves
salt
20 corncob leaves, freshly removed
30 ml (2 tbsp) ghee (page 113)

Cover the moong and urad dals with cold water and leave to soak for at least 3–4 hours. Drain and blend in a blender or food processor with the green chillies and a little water. Add the remaining ingredients, except the corn leaves and ghee, and mix thoroughly.

Grease the corn leaves with the ghee. Spread a little mixture over one leaf and place another greased leaf on top. Cook in a heavy-based pan or griddle (tawa) on both sides. Repeat with the remaining mixture. Serve hot still wrapped in the leaves. Coconut chutney (page 79) makes an excellent accompaniment.

95

CORN AND GREEN PEAS
Makai aur mutter usal

Serves: 6
Preparation time: 10 minutes
Cooking time: 5 minutes

If preferred, use frozen instead of fresh corn for this simple snack.

30 ml (2 tbsp) ghee (page 113)
1 medium onion, peeled and finely chopped
350 g (12 oz) cooked tender corn
225 g (8 oz) cooked shelled green peas
1 boiled potato, finely chopped
5–6 green chillies, finely chopped
30 ml (2 tbsp) finely chopped fresh coriander leaves
juice of 1 lemon
5 ml (1 level tsp) amchur powder
20 ml (4 level tsp) sugar
salt
50 g (2 oz) fried bread croûtons
100 g (4 oz) fried noodles
5 ml (1 tsp) finely chopped fresh coriander leaves
a dash of chilli powder

Heat the ghee in a large pan and fry the onion for 1 minute. Add the corn, green peas, potato, green chillies, coriander, lemon juice, amchur and sugar. Season with salt and cook for 2 minutes.

Turn the mixture out on to a large serving plate. Add the croûtons, noodles, coriander leaves and chilli powder. Toss and serve.

BEATEN RICE WADAS
Pohe ke wade

Serves: 4–6
Preparation time: 15–20 minutes
plus 1 hour soaking
Cooking time: 25 minutes

This delicious quick snack is suitable for any occasion. Serve with green chutney (page 106).

30 ml (2 level tbsp) moong dal
175 g (6 oz) beaten rice (pohe)
60 ml (4 tbsp) finely chopped spinach
15 ml (1 tbsp) finely chopped fresh coriander leaves
5 ml (1 tsp) lemon juice
5 ml (1 level tsp) sugar
3 green chillies, ground or finely chopped
salt
oil for deep frying

Green Chick Pea Salad (see page 77)

Cover the moong dal in cold water and leave to soak for 1 hour.

Wash the beaten rice and leave to drain for 10 minutes. Mix all the ingredients thoroughly, season with salt and shape into medium-sized balls.

Heat the oil in a deep-fat fryer (kadai) and when hot, add the balls in small batches. Cook until golden brown, remove with a slotted spoon, then drain on absorbent kitchen paper. Serve hot.

SPICY CABBAGE CAKE
Bandhgobhi wadi

This delicious cabbage cake can be served as a main dish or as a snack.

450 ml (¾ pint) thin coconut milk (page 116)
225 g (8 oz) grated cabbage
2 medium onions, peeled and finely chopped
60 ml (4 level tbsp) gram flour (besan)
2 pinches of bicarbonate of soda
30 ml (2 tbsp) oil
salt

Serves: 6–8
Preparation time: 15 minutes
Cooking time: 30 minutes

PASTE
6 green chillies
2.5 cm (1 inch) piece fresh ginger, peeled
2×2.5 cm (1 inch) cinnamon sticks
6 cloves

Grease a wide ovenproof dish and heat the oven to 180°C/350°F/Gas mark 4.

Blend the ingredients for the paste in a blender or food processor with a little water.

Mix all the remaining ingredients and pour the mixture into the prepared dish. Bake in the oven for 25–30 minutes. Cool for 5 minutes then cut into pieces and serve hot.

97

TOP *Papad Rolls (see page 94)*
BOTTOM *Moong Dal Patties (see page 93)*

SPINACH PAKODA CHAAT
◣ *Palak pakoda chaat* ◢

Serves: 6
Preparation time: 10 minutes
Cooking time: 10 minutes

If wished, the spinach can be substituted by aubergine slices dipped in the same batter and deep fried

125 g (4 oz) gram flour (besan)
2.5 ml (½ level tsp) chilli powder plus a little extra for sprinkling
150 ml (¼ pint) water
salt
oil for deep frying
10 fresh spinach leaves, shredded
30 ml (2 tbsp) sweet chutney (sonth, page 106), to serve
roasted cumin seed powder (page 118), to taste

Mix the gram flour, 2.5 ml (½ level tsp) chilli powder and the water into a batter. Season with salt.

Put the oil into a deep-fat fryer (kadai) and when hot, dip the spinach in the batter and drop a few at a time into the oil. Cook until crisp, remove with a slotted spoon, then drain on absorbent kitchen paper. Continue until all the spinach is fried.

Place the spinach pakodas on a serving plate. Spread with the sweet chutney and sprinkle with chilli powder, cumin powder and salt. Serve at once.

CORN PAKODAS
◣ *Makai pakoda* ◢

Makes 30–40 pakodas
Preparation time: 10 minutes
Cooking time: 10 minutes

Pakodas are popular fried snacks made with a variety of vegetables and lentils. If you find that they break up when frying them, add 2 teaspoons of gram flour or plain flour to the mixture.

6 tender corn on the cobs, kernels grated
15 ml (1 tbsp) finely chopped fresh coriander leaves
3 green chillies, finely chopped
salt
oil for deep frying

Mix the corn with the coriander and green chillies. Season with salt.

Heat the oil in a deep-fat fryer (kadai) and when hot, add 5 ml (1 tsp) of the mixture at a time. Cook until crisp, remove with a slotted spoon, then drain on absorbent kitchen paper to drain. Continue until all the pakodas have been cooked.

PEANUT PAKODAS
Moongphali ke pakode

The peanuts give this cocktail snack a pleasant crunchiness.

125 g (4 oz) gram flour (besan)
150 g (5 oz) roasted peanuts, roughly chopped
75 g (3 oz) finely chopped spinach
3 green chillies, finely chopped
2.5 ml (½ level tsp) garam masala (page 116)
10 ml (2 tsp) lemon juice
salt
15 ml (1 tbsp) hot oil plus oil for deep frying

Serves: 6
Preparation time: 10 minutes
Cooking time: 15 minutes

Mix the gram flour with the peanuts, spinach, green chillies, garam masala and lemon juice. Season with salt and add enough water to make a dough. Finally add the hot oil and shape into small balls.

Heat the oil for frying in a deep-fat fryer (kadai) and when hot, add a few balls at a time. Cook until golden brown, remove with a slotted spoon, then drain on absorbent kitchen paper. Continue until all the pakodas are cooked. Serve hot with tomato ketchup or chutney.

QUICK SPICY SNACK
Chapati chaat bhel

In this chaat bhel, adjust the quantity of the chutneys, yogurt and powders to suit your taste.

15–20 papadis, crushed plus 4–5 whole papadis
15 ml (1 tbsp) chopped pineapple
1 boiled potato, cubed
15 ml (1 tbsp) finely chopped raw mango
60 ml (4 tbsp) cooked white chick-peas (kabuli chane) or boiled green peas
45–60 ml (2–3 tbsp) sweet chutney (sonth) (page 106)
20–30 ml (1½–2 tbsp) green chutney (page 106)
100 ml (4 fl oz) natural yogurt (dahi, page 114)
10 ml (2 level tsp) cumin seed powder
10 ml (2 level tsp) chilli powder
10 ml (2 level tsp) chaat masala (page 119)

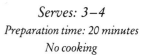

Serves: 3–4
Preparation time: 20 minutes
No cooking

Mix the crushed papadis, pineapple, potato, mango, peas, chutneys and yogurt to taste. Sprinkle over the powders and arrange a few papadis on top to serve.

POTATO SNACK
Hare masale ke aloo

Serves: 8–10
Preparation time: 5 minutes
Cooking time: 20 minutes

This potato snack is both tasty and easy to make. Serve with drinks.

8 medium-sized potatoes, peeled
22.5 ml (4½ level tsp) chaat masala (page 119)
salt

PASTE
20–30 fresh mint leaves
45 ml (3 tbsp) finely chopped fresh coriander leaves
3–4 green chillies
2.5 cm (1 inch) piece fresh ginger, peeled
5 ml (1 tsp) lemon juice

Boil the potatoes, drain and cool, then dice.
    Blend the ingredients for the paste in a blender or food processor with a little water and add the chaat masala. Season with salt and mix thoroughly. Add to the potatoes and mix in. Taste and adjust seasoning if necessary. Chill and serve cold with cocktail sticks.

VEGETABLE KEBABS
Seekh kabab

Serves: 6
Preparation time: 15 minutes
Cooking time: 40 minutes

These kebabs make an excellent dish for barbecue parties.

2 medium potatoes, peeled
100 g (4 oz) yam (jimikandh), peeled
30 ml (2 tbsp) lemon juice
30 ml (2 tbsp) finely chopped fresh coriander leaves
salt
a little oil
lemon juice to taste
chilli powder to taste
a few sliced onion, to serve

PASTE
8 garlic cloves, peeled
2.5 cm (1 inch) piece fresh ginger, peeled
6 small green chillies

Blend the ingredients for the paste in a blender or food processor with a little water.

Steam the potatoes and yam for 20–30 minutes until soft, then cool and mash into a smooth paste. Add the spice paste, lemon juice and coriander leaves. Season with salt and mix thoroughly, then divide into 12–15 portions.

Grease 12–15 skewers with oil and wrap one portion on each skewer over a length of 5–7.5 cm (2–3 inches). Brush with oil and cook directly on live coals.

Sprinkle lemon juice, chilli powder and salt to taste on the sliced onions. Serve the kebabs hot surrounded by the onions.

SEMOLINA AND VERMICELLI IDLI
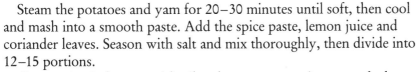
Sooji sevia idli

This popular South Indian-style snack is quick and easy to prepare.

75 ml (5 tbsp) oil
30 ml (2 tbsp) cashew nut pieces
150 g (5 oz) semolina (rawa)
275 g (10 oz) vermicelli (sevia), broken into small pieces
200 ml (⅓ pint) 2 day-old sour natural yogurt (dahi, page 114)
salt
10 ml (2 level tsp) urad dal
5 ml (1 level tsp) mustard seeds
5–6 green chillies, finely chopped
3–4 curry leaves

Serves: 4–6
Preparation time: 15 minutes
Cooking time: 30 minutes

Heat 30 ml (2 tbsp) oil in a large pan and fry the cashew nuts until golden. Remove the nuts and set aside. In the same oil, fry the semolina on a low heat until light brown in colour. Remove the semolina and set aside. Put a further 30 ml (2 tbsp) oil in the same pan. Heat and fry the vermicelli until golden in colour.

Mix the semolina, vermicelli, cashew nuts and sour yogurt and add enough water to make a batter of a dropping consistency. Season with salt.

Heat the remaining oil in a very small pan and fry the urad dal and mustard seeds. When the seeds splutter, add the green chillies and curry leaves. Add this mixture to the batter and mix well.

Spread layers of about 2 cm (¾ inch) of the mixture in ramekins or small bowls (katoris) and put into a steamer. Steam for 10 minutes. Serve hot with coconut chutney (page 79). (Indian cooks steam the mixture in a special pan called an idli vessel.)

QUICK GREEN PEA SNACK
Hare mutter ki choongi

Serves: 4
Preparation time: 15 minutes
Cooking time: 10 minutes

This tasty dish is substantial enough to serve as a main meal.

30 ml (2 tbsp) oil
550 g (1¼ lb) shelled green peas
1.25 ml (¼ level tsp) black pepper
2.5 ml (½ level tsp) chilli powder
1.25 ml (¼ level tsp) ginger powder
1.25 ml (¼ level tsp) sugar
salt
15 ml (1 tbsp) butter
5 ml (1 level tsp) amchur powder
2.5 ml (½ level tsp) roasted cumin powder (page 118)
15 ml (1 tbsp) finely chopped fresh coriander leaves
corn chips or any crisps

Heat the oil in a frying pan and add the peas, black pepper, chilli and ginger powders and sugar. Season with salt, cover and cook until the peas are tender. Add the butter, amchur and cumin powders and toss.

Remove from the heat, sprinkle the coriander leaves and corn chips on top and serve.

CABBAGE PARCELS
Bandhgobhi ghughra

Serves: 4–6
Preparation time: 40 minutes
Cooking time: 20 minutes

The raisins in these delicious stuffed pastries provide a pleasantly sweet contrast to the cabbage.

250 g (9 oz) wholemeal flour (gehun ka atta)
30 ml (2 tbsp) ghee (page 113)
2.5 ml (½ level tsp) salt
oil for deep frying

STUFFING
5 ml (1 level tsp) salt
350 g (12 oz) grated cabbage
30 ml (2 tbsp) finely chopped fresh coriander leaves
10 ml (2 tsp) lemon juice
30 ml (2 tbsp) raisins
30 ml (2 tbsp) grated fresh coconut or flaked coconut
4 green chillies, crushed or finely chopped
about 10 ml (2 level tsp) sugar
salt

Mix the wholemeal flour, the ghee and the salt. Add enough water to make a soft dough and knead thoroughly.

To make the stuffing: sprinkle the salt on the grated cabbage. Mix well and set aside. After 10 minutes, squeeze out the water by pressing with the hands. Add all the remaining ingredients, mix and season with salt.

SEMOLINA PANCAKES
Rawa uttapam

From South India, this is a dish served hot at breakfast, with coconut chutney (page 79).

200 ml (⅓ pint) natural yogurt (dahi, page 114)
100 ml (4 fl oz) water
275 g (10 oz) semolina (rawa)
salt
3 medium tomatoes, sliced
3 onions, peeled and sliced
chilli powder to taste
oil for cooking

Makes about 10
pancakes
Preparation time: 10 minutes
plus 4 hours fermentation
Cooking time: 20 minutes

Beat the yogurt with the water, then add the semolina and season with salt. If the mixture is too thick, add a little more water. The batter is better if set aside for 3–4 hours but, if in a hurry, it can be used immediately.

Spread a little batter in a hot heavy-based pan or griddle (tawa). Top with a few tomato and onion slices and sprinkle with chilli powder and salt. Pour a little oil around the sides and cook until brown on the underside, turn and cook on the other side. Repeat with the remaining batter and ingredients.

VEGETABLE PANCAKES
Karigai adai

Serves: 6–8
Preparation time: 15 minutes
plus 2 hours soaking
Cooking time: 30 minutes

This is a modified version of the popular South Indian pancake, combining rice, lentils and vegetables.

175 g (6 oz) long-grain rice
30 ml (2 level tbsp) toovar dal
30 ml (2 level tbsp) chana dal
30 ml (2 level tbsp) urad dal
8 red chillies (optional)
a pinch of asafoetida powder
45 ml (3 tbsp) grated or flaked coconut
1 medium carrot, peeled and finely chopped
75 ml (5 tbsp) cabbage, finely chopped
2 medium onions, peeled and finely chopped
75 ml (5 tbsp) finely chopped fresh coriander leaves
a few sprigs of curry leaves, finely chopped
2–3 green chillies, finely chopped
salt
oil for cooking

Cover the rice and dals in separate bowls with cold water and leave to soak for 2 hours. Drain the dals and rice and set aside the urad dal. Put the rice, toovar dal and chana dal, red chillies and asafoetida into a blender or food processor with a little water and grind to a course batter.

Add all the remaining ingredients. Season with salt and add a little water, if the batter is very thick.

Pour a ladleful of the batter at a time into a hot heavy-based frying pan or griddle (tawa) brushed with oil. Spread into a 10 cm (4 inch) round like a pancake and when small brown spots appear on the surface turn the rounds and cook on the other side. Serve hot with coconut chutney (page 79).

SEMOLINA TOAST
Rawa nasta

This quick breakfast snack combines South Indian and Western cookery. Serve hot with coconut chutney (page 79).

100 ml (4 fl oz) natural yogurt (dahi, page 114)
100 ml (4 fl oz) water
50 g (2 oz) plain flour (maida)
75 g (3 oz) semolina (rawa)
1.25 ml (¼ level tsp) baking powder
salt
15 ml (1 tbsp) finely chopped tomatoes
15 ml (1 tbsp) finely chopped onions
1.25 ml (¼ tsp) finely chopped green chillies
6 bread slices
oil or ghee (page 113)
45–60 ml (3–4 tbsp) grated cheese
a few dashes of chilli powder

Makes 6 toasts
Preparation time: 10 minutes
plus 5 hours fermentation
Cooking time: 20 minutes

Beat the yogurt with the water. Mix the flour with the semolina, baking powder and yogurt mixture. Season with salt and set the batter aside for 5 hours to ferment.

Mix the tomatoes, onions and green chillies. Dip the bread slices one at a time into the batter and cook in a heavy-based pan or griddle (tawa) lightly brushed with oil or ghee. When golden on the underside, turn the bread slices and brown on the other side. Sprinkle over a little of the tomato mixture, then a little grated cheese. Add a dash of chilli powder and season with salt. Put under the grill for 1 minute. Serve this snack hot.

SPICY SNACK CALCUTTA-STYLE
Calcutta chaat

Do not let the long list of ingredients in this recipe deter you – this spicy fruit and vegetable salad is not difficult to make.

Serves: 6–8
Preparation time: 15 minutes
plus 30 minutes soaking
Cooking time: 30 minutes

PAPADIS
250 g (9 oz) plain flour (maida)
10 ml (2 level tsp) ajwain powder
15 ml (1 tbsp) oil
2.5 ml (½ level tsp) salt
oil for deep frying

SWEET CHUTNEY (sonth)
100 g (4 oz) tamarind, seeded or 15 ml (1 tbsp) tamarind paste
75 g (3 oz) sugar
200 ml (⅓ pint) water
7.5 ml (1½ level tsp) chilli powder
5 ml (1 level tsp) cumin seed powder
2.5 ml (½ level tsp) black salt (sanchal)
5 ml (1 level tsp) salt

GREEN CHUTNEY
25 g (1 oz) finely chopped fresh coriander leaves
4 green chillies
juice of 1 lemon
2.5 ml (½ level tsp) salt
100 ml (4 fl oz) water

PAKODIS
175 g (6 oz) urad dal
75 g (3 oz) moong dal
4 green chillies
1 cm (½ inch) piece fresh ginger, peeled
5 ml (1 level tsp) nigella seeds (kalonji)
1.25 ml (¼ level tsp) asafoetida powder
salt
oil for frying

FOR SERVING
450 ml (¾ pint) natural yogurt (dahi, page 114)
salt
2 medium potatoes, boiled and sliced
chaat masala (page 119), cumin seed powder, chilli powder, to taste

First cover the urad dal and the moong dal for the pakodis, in cold water and leave to soak for 3–4 hours.

To make the papadis: mix the plain flour, ajwain, oil and salt and add enough water to make a soft dough. Knead well and roll out into small thin rounds about 4 cm (1½ inches) in diameter, without using flour if possible. Prick with a fork.

Heat the oil for frying in a deep-fat fryer (kadai) and when hot, add the papadis in small batches. Cook until golden brown, remove with a slotted spoon then drain on absorbent kitchen paper.

Continue until all the papadis have been cooked. To make the sweet chutney (sonth): put the tamarind paste on to boil with the sugar and water. Boil for 15 minutes, then mash and strain. Add the chilli and cumin seed powders and the salts. Store in the refrigerator.

To make the green chutney: put the coriander leaves, green chillies, lemon juice, salt and the water into a blender and blend to a smooth paste. Store in the refrigerator.

TO MAKE THE PAKODIS

Drain the urad and moong dal and put into a blender with the chillies and ginger and blend with a little water. Add the nigella seeds (kalonji) and asafoetida powder. Season with salt and shape into small balls.

Heat the oil in a deep-fat fryer (kadai) and when hot, add the balls in small batches. Cook until golden brown, remove with a slotted spoon, and drain on absorbent kitchen paper. Continue until all the pakodis have been cooked. Soak the fried pakodis in water. After 30 minutes, squeeze out the water and set the pakodis aside.

To serve, beat the yogurt with a little salt. On each serving plate, place 3–4 pakodis, 2–3 potato slices and a few pakodis all dipped in sweet chutney (sonth). Sprinkle with a little green chutney and yogurt, chaat masala, cumin seed powder, chilli powder and salt.

DRINKS

Cooling drinks are obviously necessary in a hot country like India. Sherbets using typical Indian flavours like rose, khus-khus (poppy seeds), and chandan (sandalwood paste) are also very cooling, but their popularity has declined recently.

Among the simple low-cost drinks, perhaps one of the most popular is neembu pani. This refreshing drink is extremely simple to make - mix lemon juice and sugar to taste with water. A little more zest can be added by using soda or lemonade in place of water and, if lemon juice is not available, lemon squash can be used instead.

Another cooling drink is lassi or buttermilk, which is made by churning natural yogurt with water. For sweet lassi, sugar is added whereas for savoury lassi, salt and seasoning (like cumin seed powder) is used. In many parts of the country, salted buttermilk is drunk with the mid-day meal.

The most popular hot drink is tea and a wide variety of masala teas are also prepared. In the South, however, coffee is preferred and many households roast their own beans and make percolated coffee.

LIME CUP
Kesari sherbet

Lemon juice, ginger and rose syrup transform sweet lime juice into a delectable drink.

1.1 litre (2 pints) sweet lime juice
30 ml (2 tbsp) rose syrup
20 ml (4 tsp) lemon juice
5 ml (1 tsp) ginger juice
crushed ice

Serves: 6
*Preparation time: a few
minutes*
No cooking

Mix all the ingredients, except the ice, and leave to chill. Serve in tall glasses with lots of crushed ice.

SPICY MILK SHAKE
Thandai

This cooling drink, with its true oriental flavour, tastes even better if the spices are ground with a pestle and mortar.

100 g (4 oz) poppy seeds (khus-khus)
225 g (8 oz) almonds
15 ml (1 level tbsp) aniseed (saunf)
30 ml (2 level tbsp) ginger powder
5 ml (1 level tsp) ground pepper
275 g (10 oz) sugar
300 ml (½ pint) water

Makes 10–12 glasses
*Preparation time: a few
minutes*
No cooking

TO SERVE
900 ml–1.1 litres (1½–2 pints) cold milk
900 ml–1.1 litres (1½–2 pints) cold water

Blend the poppy seeds, almonds, aniseed, ginger powder, pepper and sugar with the water in a blender or food processor. Strain, bottle and store the syrup in the refrigerator.

To serve, put 22.5 ml (4½ tsp) of the syrup into a glass, add 90 ml (6 tbsp) of the milk and 90 ml (6 tbsp) of the water. Stir to mix, taste and add a little more syrup if a sweeter drink is preferred. Make up the other glasses in the same way. Serve chilled.

SAFFRON CUP
Kesar sherbet

For this unusual and refreshing drink, adjust the amount of sugar to taste.

4–5 strands saffron or 2 pinches of saffron powder
15 ml (1 tbsp) warm water
60 ml (4 tbsp) lemon juice
90 ml (6 level tbsp) sugar
1.25 ml (¼ level tsp) cardamom powder
1.25 ml (¼ level tsp) salt
1.1 litres (2 pints) water
crushed ice

Put the saffron into a small bowl with the warm water and rub until it dissolves. Transfer the saffron water to a larger bowl and add all the remaining ingredients except the ice. Leave to chill. Pour into glasses and serve with lots of crushed ice.

VARIATION

SAFFRON SANDALWOOD DRINK
Kesar chandan sherbet

To each glass of kesar sherbet, add 1.25 ml (¼ level tsp) of chandan (a yellowish paste obtained by hand-rubbing sandalwood with a little water in a pestle and mortar or on a flat surface). Chandan is known for its pleasantly cooling effect and it is widely used in Hindu and Jain religious ceremonies.

KASHMIRI TEA
Kahva

Makes 3 cups
Preparation time: a few
minutes
Cooking time: a few minutes

Kashmiris are very fond of tea and drink two varieties: one a dark red-brown, salty variety which is served with cream and the other, a delicately flavoured sweet tea known as kahva. A special variety of tea is used for making kahva but as it is not available outside of Kashmir, try this version made with green tea. Chinese tea can also be used. Kashmiris store kahva in a samovar which keeps it hot and serve it in small decorative metal cups which are tinned on the inside.

400 ml (⅔ pint) boiling water
10 ml (2 level tsp) green tea
2 pinches of saffron (optional)
2.5 ml (½ tsp) warm water
seeds of 2 cardamoms, lightly crushed
4 almonds, blanched and chopped
1 cm (½ inch) piece of cinnamon
1 clove
15 ml (1 level tbsp) sugar

In a saucepan, pour the water over the tea and leave to infuse over a very low heat.

Meanwhile, put the saffron into a bowl with the 2.5 ml (½ tsp) water and rub until it dissolves. Strain the tea and add the saffron liquid together with all the other ingredients. Reheat and serve at once.

BASIC RECIPES

Certain recipes are fundamental to Indian cooking, and these are included on the following pages. In some cases (for example, the Saambhar powder), the amounts of the spices within the recipe can be varied according to taste.

TOP *Agar Agar Sweet (see page 91)*
BOTTOM *Pistachio Barfi (see page 88)*

CLARIFIED BUTTER
Ghee

BASIC RECIPES

Ghee, traditionally used in Indian cooking, is a fat made from butter.
In tropical climates, butter goes rancid quickly but, in contrast, ghee,
which is made by clarifying butter, can be preserved at room
temperature for long periods. Stored in the refrigerator, it can be kept
almost indefinitely. In winter or at low temperatures, ghee sets into a
milky white or slightly yellowish solid.

450 g (1 lb) unsalted butter

Melt the butter in a saucepan over medium heat and simmer gently for
about 25 minutes. During this period, a sediment should separate out
and settle at the bottom leaving a clear yellow liquid at the top.

  Remove from the heat and let the liquid cool a little. Carefully strain
the clarified liquid through a muslin cloth or metal sieve lined with
muslin into a container with a close-fitting cover, taking care not to
disturb the sediment. Cover tightly and store.

*Makes about 350 g
(12 oz) ghee*
*Preparation time: a few
minutes*
Cooking time: 25 minutes

CORIANDER-CUMIN SEED POWDER
Dhana-jira powder

This simple mixture of spices is widely used in Gujarat as a masala for
vegetable dishes.

350 g (12 oz) coriander seeds
100 g (4 oz) cumin seeds

Dry roast the seeds on a low heat in a heavy-based saucepan until they
give out an aroma. Remove from the heat and grind in a small coffee or
electric grinder or with a mortar and pestle. Sieve the mixture and, if
required, grind the coarse portion again. Store in an airtight container
in a cool dry place.

Makes 400 g (14 oz)
*Preparation time: a few
minutes*
Cooking time: 5–7 minutes

113

LEFT *Kashmiri Tea (see page 111)*
RIGHT *Lime Cup (see page 109)*

NATURAL YOGURT
◼ *Dahi* ◼

Makes 600 ml (1 pint)
yogurt
Preparation time: a few
minutes
Setting time: overnight
or 8–10 hours

Natural yogurt is made by adding a small quantity of yogurt to warmed milk, the bacteria contained in the yogurt then reproduce themselves. The temperature of the milk is crucial (43°C/110°F) to this procedure – if too hot, it will kill the 'starter' yogurt; if too cool, the bacteria won't work.

In a warm climate such as that of India (where, incidentally, many families make yogurt daily), the mixture can be left to set in a bowl. In colder climates, a wide-necked vacuum flask is a better idea. The yogurt should be left for a period of 8–10 hours and the container should not be touched during that time as movement disturbs the setting process. By increasing the quantity of natural yogurt added, the setting time is reduced. Once you start making yogurt at home, remember to set aside in the refrigerator about 30 ml (2 tbsp) as a starter for the next batch you make.

600 ml (1 pint) milk
30 ml (2 tbsp) natural yogurt (dahi)

Boil the milk in a saucepan. Cool until lukewarm and pour into a warm heatproof bowl or vacuum flask. Add the yogurt and mix. Cover the bowl with a tea-cosy and leave in a warm place, for instance the oven at its lowest setting. If using a vacuum flask, close securely. Leave undisturbed overnight or for 8–10 hours until set.

When set, store in the refrigerator and use when required.

SOFT CHEESE
◼ *Paneer* ◼

Makes 175 g (6 oz)
paneer
Preparation time: 10 minutes
No cooking

Paneer is a nutritious, home-made soft cheese which can be used in many dishes: with vegetables, in parathas, and for snacks and sweets, it can also be eaten by itself. The liquid, or whey, strained from paneer can be reserved and used instead of water for making soups, stocks and gravies. The soft cheese which separates from the milk is known as chhanna. This is usually pressed and sold in slabs when it is described as 'pressed paneer'.

1 litre (1¾ pints) milk
10 ml (2 tsp) fresh lemon juice

Heat the milk in a saucepan and bring slowly to the boil. Gradually, add the lemon juice, stirring constantly. Continue to stir gently until the milk curdles and separates. Set aside to cool for a few minutes to allow the paneer to set, then strain it through a muslin-lined sieve. Squeeze out the remaining liquid (whey) from the solids.

For pressed paneer: wrap a layer of cheese about 2.5 cm (1 inch) thick in muslin or a clean cloth. Place on a work surface and weight down for at least 1 hour. Cut into rectangular pieces or use as directed in the recipes.

VARIATION

For a lightly salted paneer, add 5 ml (1 level tsp) salt with 200 ml (⅓ pint) natural yogurt. Do not add lemon juice.

SAAMBHAR POWDER

The basic proportions added for this mixture are given, below, but they can be varied according to taste for a hotter or milder effect.

oil for cooking
450 g (1 lb) red chillies
15–20 dried curry leaves (optional)
450 g (1 lb) coriander seeds
100 g (4 oz) cumin seeds
50 g (2 oz) mustard seeds
25 g (1 oz) fenugreek seeds (methi)
25 g (1 oz) black peppercorns
50 g (2 oz) chana dal
50 g (2 oz) toovar dal
25 g (1 oz) urad dal
175 g (6 oz) rice
100 g (4 oz) turmeric powder
50 g (2 oz) sesame seeds

Makes 1.5 kg (3 lbs)
Preparation time: 5 minutes
Cooking time: 5 minutes

Heat a little oil in a heavy-based pan or griddle (tawa) and fry the chillies. Remove from the pan and add a little more oil and fry the curry leaves until crisp. Remove and set aside.

Wipe the pan and dry-fry all the other ingredients until crisp.

Grind all the ingredients in a coffee grinder or with a mortar and pestle. Sieve and store in an airtight container.

115

COCONUT MILK
Nariyal ka doodh

Coconut milk, which forms the basis of many dishes from the State of Kerala and of Sri Lanka, can be thick or thin. The quantities given here are approximate because coconuts yield a varying amount of flesh.

Moreover, since there are slight variations from recipe to recipe, follow the quantities of liquid and thickness required as given in the individual recipes.

Makes coconut milk equal to quantity of water used
Preparation time: 15 minutes plus soaking time (15 minutes for thick milk)
No cooking

Basic quantities
100 ml (4 fl oz) water for thick milk plus 750 ml (1¼ pint) for thin milk
1 large coconut, flesh removed and grated

Add the 100 ml (4 fl oz) water to the coconut and leave to soak for about 15 minutes. Squeeze out the milk from the flesh with your hands into a bowl.

This milk, from the first extraction, is called thick milk. Set aside the grated flesh for a second extraction yielding thin coconut milk. To make thin milk: add 750 ml (1¼ pint) water to the squeezed-out coconut. Blend in a mixer or food processor and strain through a muslin-lined sieve.

If no thick milk is required, the grated coconut can be used without preliminary extraction and blended with water.

VARIATION
Coconut milk can also be made with solid creamed coconut (available in Indian food stores and large supermarkets). Dissolve it in warm water, stirring constantly. For thick coconut milk use 50 g (2 oz) creamed coconut to 100 ml (4 fl oz) warm water and for thin coconut milk make the water part up to 750 ml (1¼ pint).

MIXED SPICES
Garam masala

Garam masala, literally 'hot spices', is a general term used for a combination of anything from 3–15 ground spices. It is used in cooking to give a nice warm feeling when the dish is eaten. Irrespective of the type of garam masala, cinnamon and cloves are always present; the next most common ingredients are black peppercorns and cardamoms.

Commercially prepared garam masala is readily available but the home-made is preferable because spices lose their aroma and flavour so quickly. Even when preparing masala at home, it is best to make small

Makes 30 ml (2 tbsp)
Preparation time: a few minutes
Cooking time: a few minutes

BASIC RECIPES

quantities and to store any extra in an airtight container for only a brief period of time.

The following recipe is based on the Punjabi style of garam masala. You can, however, use any other combination you like for instance, an equal number of cinnamon sticks, cloves and peppercorns.

2×2.5 cm (1 inch) cinnamon sticks
6 cloves
12 black peppercorns
seeds of 4 cardamoms
10 ml (2 level tsp) cumin seeds
3 bay leaves

Dry roast all the spices together over a gentle heat in a heavy-based frying pan. Stir constantly until they are lightly coloured and give out a strong aroma. Remove from the heat and grind in a small coffee or electric grinder or with a mortar and pestle. Store in an airtight container.

PAAON BHAJI MASALA
Paaon bhaji masala

This masala is used not only for paaon bhaji but also in making other vegetable dishes and for sprinkling on dry mixtures.

30 ml (2 level tbsp) chilli powder
15 ml (1 level tbsp) coriander-cumin seed powder (dhana-jira, page 113)
15 ml (1 level tbsp) roasted cumin seed powder (page 118)
5 ml (1 level tsp) mustard seeds
5 ml (1 level tsp) garlic powder (optional)
8 cloves
8 black peppercorns

Makes 75 ml (5 level tbsp)
Preparation time: a few minutes
Cooking time: a few minutes

Grind all the ingredients in a coffee grinder to a powder. Store in an airtight container in a cool dry place.

117

TAMARIND WATER
Imli ka rus

Tamarind water is a very common ingredient in South Indian cookery.

30 ml (2 tbsp) tamarind pods or 15 ml (1 tbsp) tamarind paste
150 ml (¼ pint) warm water

Makes 150 ml (¼ pint)
Preparation time: 20 minutes
No cooking

Soak the tamarind pods in the warm water for about 15 minutes to soften the pulp. Mix thoroughly and squeeze the tamarind so as to obtain as concentrated a juice as possible. Strain through a sieve. Reserve the strained water for use in recipes. Store the juice in a screw-topped jar in the refrigerator.

ROASTED CUMIN SEED POWDER
Bhoona jira

The true flavour of cumin emerges when they are dry roasted then finely ground.

Makes 100 g (4 oz)
Preparation time: a few
minutes
Cooking time: a few minutes

100 g (4 oz) cumin seeds

Dry roast the cumin seeds in a hot, heavy-based pan or griddle (tawa). Cool and grind to a powder in a small coffee or electric grinder or with a pestle and mortar. Sieve the mixture and, if required, grind the coarse portion again. Store in an airtight container in a cool dry place.

MILK CONCENTRATE
Khoya

Khoya or mawa is the solid residue obtained after milk has been boiled for about 45 minutes. It is the basis for the preparation of a large number of Indian sweets and, being a rich ingredient, is also used in preparing expensive vegetable dishes. The quantity of khoya obtained will vary depending upon the fat content of the milk. Use full-fat milk to get the best khoya in the shortest time.

Makes about 300 ml
(½ pint)
Preparation time: a few
minutes
Cooking time: about 45
minutes

1.1 litres (2 pints) milk

Bring the milk to the boil in a large heavy-based saucepan, preferably non-stick. Lower the heat and simmer, stirring frequently. In about 40–45 minutes, the milk should have been reduced to a quarter of its original volume, the entire mass becoming a soft ball of sticky dough.

Remove with the help of a spatula. Cool and store in the refrigerator. For longer periods deep freeze.

VARIATION

Another method of obtaining khoya is to boil 100 ml (4 fl oz) milk to which 350 g (12 oz) of powdered milk has been added. Blend in 30 ml (2 tbsp) butter and remove from the heat.

CHAAT MASALA
Chaat masala

A spicy, piquant masala combining salty, tart and pungent tastes, it is widely used in chaats and other snacks.

50 g (2 oz) coriander seeds, slightly dry roasted
25 g (1 oz) red chillies
100 g (4 oz) roasted cumin seed powder (page 118)
50 g (2 oz) amchur powder
30 ml (2 level tbsp) black peppercorns
30 ml (2 level tbsp) black salt (sanchal)
300 g (11 oz) salt

Makes 550 g (1¼ lbs)
Preparation time: a few
minutes
Cooking time: a few minutes

Grind all the ingredients together in a coffee grinder to a powder. Store in an airtight container in a cool dry place.

SPROUTING PULSES

The technique used below can be used to sprout a variety of pulses.

175 g (6 oz) dried pulses

Makes about 275 g
(10 oz)
Preparation time: 5 minutes
plus about 24 hours soaking
and sprouting

Put the pulses into a bowl, cover with cold water and leave to soak overnight. Drain the pulses and tie loosely in a piece of cloth until they sprout.

Alternatively, put into a colander and cover with a wet cloth. After 6 hours, sprinkle over a little water and cover again with the wet cloth.

Depending upon the pulse, sprouts will appear after 12–18 hours.

GLOSSARY OF INGREDIENTS

The glossary is divided into five sections namely Herbs and Spices; Fruits and Vegetables; Pulses and Dals; Flours; and Other Ingredients.

HERBS AND SPICES

With few exceptions, the Indian housewife makes her own fresh spice mixtures which are known as masalas. In the case of garam masala (page 116), there are innumerable masala combinations to suit individual tastes and to bring out different flavours. The reason for making fresh masalas is that ground spices lose their fragrance and the aroma of natural oils at a fairly rapid rate. If ground spices or masalas are used, take care to make or buy only small quantities and store in an airtight container.

AJWAIN   Ajwain is a spice which also has highly digestive properties and is used to relieve flatulence and minor stomach aches. The seeds, which belong to the caraway family, are small and light brown in colour and have a bitter flavour. Ajwain does not have an equivalent name in English but is sometimes sold under its botanical name *carum*.

ANISEED OR FENNEL SEEDS (*saunf*) These highly aromatic spices taste and smell like liquorice. The thin, elongated seeds are pale green or light brown in colour and are considered to have digestive properties. In many parts of India they are chewed after meals to aid digestion, and to act as a breath freshener.

ASAFOETIDA (*hing*)   This strong spice is the resin of a plant. It is sold both in its root form and as a powder, the latter being the more convenient form to use. Asafoetida has a distinctive, pungent flavour and aroma, largely due to the presence of sulphur compounds and is, therefore, used in very small quantitites. It has strong digestive properties and is used to counteract flatulence. It is an essential ingredient in Gujarati, Maharashtran, Kashmiri and South Indian cooking; it is, however, rarely used in the North.

TEJ PATTA   Tej patta is the leaf of the cassia tree, whose bark has the flavour of cinnamon (and is often sold as such). It is important to use only tender young leaves which are full of flavour. Bay leaves are the Western equivalent of the Indian tej patta.

BLACK PEPPER (*kali mirch*)   See under Peppercorns.

CARDAMOMS (*illaichi*)   Cardamoms are generally divided into two types: small and large. In home cooking, the small cardamoms are the most commonly used. There are two varieties, namely the stronger flavoured green cardamoms and the lesser flavoured bleached white cardamoms. You can use whichever type of smaller cardamoms are available but will naturally have to consider the need to make marginal adjustments in quantities. The large cardamoms are coarser in texture, and although they have a stronger flavour, also have a slightly bitter taste. Being more economical in cost, they are widely used in hotels and restaurants. Although the entire cardamom, including husk, can be used in cooking, by and large it is the black or dark brown seeds, with their pungent and highly aromatic flavour, which are used. In fact, cardamoms are almost always an ingredient in garam masalas (page 116). They are also among the few spices to be used both in spicy dishes and in sweets.

Cardamoms are considered to have digestive properties and are often brewed along with other spices in teas and used to clear sore throats and colds. They are also chewed after meals both as a digestive and as a breath sweetener.

CHILLIES, GREEN (*hari mirch*)   The fiery taste of green chillies is derived mainly from the tiny white seeds inside them and, to a much lesser extent, from the skin. In fact, in most cases, the skin itself has a very pleasant flavour.

One way to reduce the heat and pungency of green chillies is to remove the seeds after slitting, to rub inside with a little salt and then to wash thoroughly. Salted and pickled green chillies are therefore generally much easier on the tongue. Of course, in many parts of India, chillies are eaten raw but such a practice is not recommended for Westerners.

Fresh green chillies are firm and shiny and they should be stored in plastic bags in the refrigerator. Remember to wash your hands and not to touch your eyes after handling chillies.

CHILLIES, RED (*lal mirch*) CHILLI POWDER (*pisi hui mirch*) Dried red chillies are either sold whole or in ground form as chilli powder. The ground chilli powder is used in small quantitites as it has a more concentrated effect.

When chillies are ripe, they are usually red. Red Kashmiri chillies are darker in colour and not as hot as other whole red chillies. They are mainly used for making the dish more colourful; and if not available, ordinary whole red chillies can be substituted.

CINNAMON (*dalchini*) Cinnamon is the brownish aromatic bark of the cinnamon tree. Actually, the bark of two different trees is sold as cinnamon: that sold as the bark of the cassia tree is not true cinnamon, although its taste is very similar. Freshly ground cinnamon is an essential ingredient of garam masala (page 116). It is also chewed after meals as a breath sweetener.

CLOVES (*laung*) Cloves are the dried flower buds of the clove tree. They have a strong aromatic flavour and are invariably used in garam masalas (page 116). Good cloves should not only be well formed but also be plump and oily. Clove oil has analgesic qualitites and is a well-known remedy for toothaches.

CORIANDER LEAVES (*hara dhania, kothmir*) The fresh green leaves of the coriander plant, which belongs to the parsley family, are very widely used as a garnish in Indian cooking. Coriander leaves are, incidentally, one of the cheapest herbs sold in the market as the plant is very easy to grow and can be grown even in a small box or pot in the house. The leaves give out a fragrant flavour when they are crushed or chopped.

CORIANDER SEEDS (*dhania/dhaniya*) Coriander seeds are derived from the coriander plant. The round, light brown seeds give out a very pleasant aroma when lightly dry roasted and ground into a fine powder.

CUMIN, WHITE (*safed jira*) There are two basic varieties of cumin: white (safed jira) and black (shah jira, kala jira). As in the case of coriander seeds, the flavour and aroma emerge best after they have been dry roasted or, for that matter, added to hot oil. It is important to ensure that the temperature is high enough to make the seeds splutter and pop, otherwise the full flavour will not be released. Cumin seeds of both types are frequently used in making garam masalas (page 116). Whole black seeds are generally used in dishes such as pullavs.

CURRY LEAVES (*curry patta, meethe neem ke patte*) Curry leaves are thin, shiny and dark green in colour and are used for the aroma they release after being lightly fried in hot oil for a few seconds. They can also be dried and stored in an airtight jar until needed; but the flavour will not be as good as that of fresh leaves.

FENNEL SEEDS (*saunf*) See under Aniseed.

FENUGREEK LEAVES (*methi bhaji, hari methi*) Fenugreek leaves have a slightly bitter flavour, but are not as strong as fenugreek seeds. They are used both as a herb and a vegetable.

FENUGREEK SEEDS (*methi dane*) Fenugreek seeds are small, cylindrical and light brown or mustard in colour. The seeds are very bitter and are used, in small amounts, for tempering (vaghar) and South Indian masalas.

GARLIC (*lasun*) Because of its extremely pungent flavour, garlic is used in small quantities as a flavouring agent. It has medicinal properties and is used in indigenous medicine.

GINGER, FRESH (*adrak*) Fresh root ginger is widely used in Indian cooking. In certain parts of the country, it is served, with a little lemon juice and salt, as an accompaniment.

GINGER, DRY (*sonth*) Powdered ginger is widely used in cooking, particularly in areas like Kashmir.

MANGO POWDER, DRIED (*amchur powder*) This is made by drying small segments of unripe mango and then grinding them into a powder. It is used to give a slightly sour tangy taste to dishes. Ready-made powder is available in some shops.

MUSTARD SEEDS (*sarson, rai*) Mustard seeds are available in different colours: black, brown and white, but they have to be fried quickly in very hot oil to obtain their full flavour. In North India and Bengal, the oil from mustard seeds is used for pickles, to which it gives a slightly sharp taste.

NUTMEG (*jaiphal*) Nutmeg is the kernel of the fruit of an evergreen tree native to Indonesia. The fruit is surrounded by a case which, when dried, yields another spice known as mace (javetri).

ONION/NIGELLA SEEDS (*kalonji*) Small and triangular-shaped, the hard black seeds belong to the onion family. Apart from general cooking, they are usually used in pickles.

PEPPERCORNS, BLACK (*kali mirch*) A common ingredient in masalas, these are also regarded as a digestive and stimulant.

POPPY SEEDS (*khus-khus*) Very tiny seeds whose colour varies from creamy white to grey, they are largely used as a thickener.

SAFFRON (*zaffran, kesar*) Saffron, the most expensive spice in the world, is, in fact, the dried stamen of a crocus. It is a highly aromatic spice which gives a yellowish orange colour to dishes and is used in small quantities after being dissolved in a little warm water or milk.

SESAME SEEDS (*til, gingelly*) Small creamy white seeds, the oil of which is used for cooking in many parts of Western India.

TAMARIND (*imli*) The seed pod of the tamarind tree is soaked in warm water to extract the watery pulp and then to make tamarind water which has a sour and piquant taste (page 118). The tamarind paste, made from tamarind seeds, is more convenient to use than the pods.

TURMERIC POWDER (*haldi*) This colourful yellow powder is used not only in cooking but also in Hindu religious ceremonies. It is also used as a digestive and antiseptic.

FRUITS AND VEGETABLES

AUBERGINE/EGGPLANT (*baigan*) The aubergine is a native vegetable of India but is now widely available all over the world. Aubergines come in various shades of pink, purple, green and white, and in varying sizes and shapes, with a soft white flesh and tiny edible seeds. The common variety is usually glossy purple-black. They should be firm and shiny.

CHIKOO This is a common Indian fruit containing brown flesh and black, inedible seeds. As there is no Western equivalent, it can be omitted from the recipes.

DRUMSTICK (*saunjane ki phali*) The long ridged pods of this vegetable contain a firm but soft greyish white pulp with seeds. The pods are cut into shorter lengths and used in cooking without splitting. Omit if not available.

GUAVA (*amrud, amrood*) This green or yellow coloured fruit has a thin edible skin with a delicious cream or pink inner flesh. The small hard seeds are edible but should preferably be removed.

MANGO (*aam*) India produces a very wide variety of mangoes. Raw, unripe mangoes are used for making chutneys and pickles – the skin and the large kernel are discarded for chutneys whereas, for pickles, only the kernel is removed.

The alphonso variety of ripe mango is considered the best. Both mango slices and mango juice or purée are available in cans.

MARROW (*lauki*) This is a long vegetable, shaped somewhat like a bell. Its thin greenish-white skin has to be peeled off before the white flesh can be used for cooking.

RADISH, WHITE (*mooli*) White radishes are long, white tube-shaped vegetables. They can be eaten raw or cooked but are best eaten young, before they become woody. Because of their pungent taste, they are frequently used as a stuffing for parathas.

SWEET LIME (*mosambi*) A citrus fruit of the size of an orange, with a thick, inedible yellow skin. The sweet, yellowish-white inner fruit is encased inside a membrane which should be discarded along with the seeds. In season, the juice of the fruit is sold on wayside stalls.

SWEET POTATO (*shakarkand*) This tuberous vegetable has a thick, reddish-pink outer skin and yellowish or white flesh which has a sweet and slightly perfumed flavour. It is cooked in the same way as ordinary potatoes.

YAM (*jimikandh*) This tuberous root vegetable has a dirty brown skin with off-white or pale pink flesh. The vegetable is hard when raw and has a bland flavour when cooked.

PULSES AND DALS

Dal is the collective name for dried pulses. However, because many Indian pulses do not have Western equivalents, a problem arises regarding the terminology used. The terms chick pea, gram, lentil, pulse etc are defined in the Chambers 20th Century Dictionary in a generic sense. At the same time, from among the various Indian pulses, this dictionary lists only the terms 'mung' and 'urd'. Accordingly, the arrangement under this grouping is made not in alphabetical order of the English terms but the corresponding order of the Indian terms, the nearest English equivalent term being given in parenthesis where available.

CHANA (*yellow chick pea/Bengal gram*) The individual grams have a distinctive irregular shape. They are also sometimes called horse gram (because horses love them). The yellow dried chick peas have an outer dark brown covering and have a slightly nutty flavour. These are sold on the streets by mobile vendors and are very popular as a light snack. Many Hindus consider it auspicious to eat chane on Fridays.

They can be sprouted and used in salads and mixed pulse dishes.

HARE CHANE (*green chick peas*) These are sold both as fresh and dried. For the recipes in this book, use the dried variety.

CHANA DAL (*husked split yellow chick peas*) This is often confused with split yellow chick peas. Chana dal is the husked and split yellow chick pea. It is deep yellow in colour.

BHUJE HOOEY CHANE KI DAL (*roasted and puffed split yellow chick peas*) This is the split yellow chick pea after roasting.

KABULI CHANE/CHHOLE (*white chick peas/garbanzos*)   These hard creamish white peas double in size when soaked. Boiled and cooked white chick peas are used in salads and dals.

LOBHIA (*black-eyed beans*)   These creamy white, large oblong beans are called black-eyed beans because each bean literally has a black dot or eye in the middle. It is preferable to soak them for 4–5 hours before cooking.

MASOOR (*red lentils*)   These pinkish lentils (sometimes called Egyptian lentils) do not require soaking and are easy to cook.

MASOOR DAL (*skinned and split red lentils*) This is obtained by splitting masoor.

MATH/MOATH   There is no English equivalent for this Indian bean. The small slightly elongated brown beans have a strong nutty flavour. They require soaking and long cooking to become tender. Sprouted math is also used in salads and vegetables.

MOONG/MUNG BEAN   The English and Indian names of this versatile green bean are identical, the Indian name having been absorbed in the English language. The sprouts of this bean are widely used in Oriental cuisines. There are three types available:

SAABAT MOONG (*whole moong beans*) These beans can be boiled without soaking, and should be boiled in plenty of salted water until the skin splits and the bean is tender.

MOONG DAL (*split moong*)   The pale yellowish coloured dal is obtained by splitting moong beans after removal of skin. They generally require no soaking and can be easily cooked. Moong dal is light and easy to digest.

MOONG DAL CHILKE WALI (*split moong dal with skin*)   These beans need to be soaked for about one hour and then boiled in spiced water until tender.

RAJMA (*red kidney beans*) These somewhat large beans are available in colours ranging from light pink to dark red. It is necessary to soak them for 8–10 hours until they are double in size before cooking. Because they contain a poisonous resin which is not destroyed by light cooking, they must be boiled for at least 10 minutes before cooking as specified in recipes.

TOOVAR DAL (*arhar*)   For this dal also, there is no exact English equivalent. This yellowish coloured split bean is widely used for cooking in Northern and Western India. It is easy to digest and to cook.

URAD DAL (*black lentils/black gram*)   This is a tough black coloured dal which is very popular in South Indian cooking. These can be divided into three categories:

SAABAT URAD (*whole urad*)   These require long cooking for the skin to split and the bean to tenderise.

URAD DAL CHILKE WALI (*split urad dal with skin*)   These take less time to cook than the whole urad. During cooking, a glutinous liquid is released which gives the dal a creamy consistency.

DHULI HUI URAD DAL (*split dal without skins*)   These require even less cooking time, but need to be soaked for one hour before cooking.

FLOURS

CORNFLOUR This typically Western product, made from finely ground gram, is used at times as a thickening agent in modern Indian cuisine.

GRAM FLOUR (*besan*) The flour made from Bengal gram after removal of skin is called besan. It is widely used in Indian cooking, particularly snacks.

WHEAT FLOUR The three varieties of wheat flour used in this book are:

PLAIN FLOUR (*maida*) This is fine, all-purpose flour (the variety which is invariably used for making cakes and pastries).

SEMOLINA (*rawa*) This is a coarsely ground flour, also known as cream of wheat.

WHOLEMEAL FLOUR (*gehun ka atta*) The 'atta' or flour used for making the soft and pliable Indian breads like chapatis and parathas is very finely ground wholewheat flour. Wholemeal (also termed wholewheat or wheatmeal) flour is the best substitute because it has just enough bran in it to give it body without at the same time making it too coarse. If (gehun ka) atta or chapati flour happens to be available at a nearby Asian grocer, do use it.

NOTE Other flours such as rice flour, maize flour, moong dal flour, urad dal flour etc are also used in Indian cooking though no recipes using these have been included in this book.

OTHER INGREDIENTS

AGAR AGAR/CHINA GRASS This gelling agent is often used in India because unlike gelatine, it is a vegetarian product.

BLACK SALT (*sanchal*) This blackish-white salt is very tasty and is used in a number of savoury Indian dishes of Rajasthan and in the chaats of North India.

GHEE (*clarified butter*) This preparation goes back to the days long before refrigerators. A traditional method of preserving milk was to churn it into butter and then clarify it into ghee. Clarified butter is not only less likely to go rancid but it can also be heated to a high temperature without the risk of burning.

KEWADA ESSENCE Kewada is a typical Indian flavouring agent obtained from a special tree. If this essence is not available, it can be omitted or the alternative essence specified can be used instead.

JAGGERY (*gur*) In India, a good proportion of the sugar cane crop is used for making jaggery instead of white sugar. Basically, it is a solid lump of unrefined sugar with a unique flavour. There is really no equivalent for jaggery.

PISTACHIO NUTS (*pista*) Pistachio nuts have a hard, creamy-beige coloured shell with bright green kernels covered with purple skins. The shell splits when the kernels are ripe. They can be eaten roasted and salted as snacks, or used unroasted and unsalted in savoury and sweet dishes.

POPPADOMS (*papads/papardum*) Several varieties of papads are available in India. While the most common ones are those made from moong dal and urad dal, papads are also made from rice, potatoes and combinations of different pulses and vegetables,
   Moong dal papads are thinner and can be kept for long periods without spoiling. In contrast, urad dal papads tend to lose their freshness and flavour after some time and are best eaten fresh.

ROSE WATER (*gulab ka pani*) Rose water is liquid flavouring distilled from the rose petals. It is used to flavour Indian sweetmeats and desserts.

VARK/VARAK (*silver leaf*) Vark is real silver leaf and is used for decorating both sweet and savoury dishes; despite being a precious metal, it is edible. Vark is made by placing minute silver pellets between sheets of tissue paper. This is then enclosed in a leather pouch and flattened by beating with a hammer until the pellets are paper thin sheets.

INDEX

INDEX